D1519879

AND HE IS LIFTED UP

BOOKS BY SUZANNE DE DIETRICH
Published by The Westminster Press

AND HE IS LIFTED UP
Meditations on the Gospel of John

TOWARD FULLNESS OF LIFE
Studies in the Letter of Paul to the Philippians

FREE MEN
Meditations on the Bible Today

GOD'S UNFOLDING PURPOSE
A Guide to the Study of the Bible

THE WITNESSING COMMUNITY
The Biblical Record of God's Purpose

And He Is Lifted Up

MEDITATIONS ON THE GOSPEL OF JOHN

by

Suzanne de Dietrich

Translated by Dennis Pardee

THE WESTMINSTER PRESS

PHILADELPHIA

STANDARD BOOK NO. 664–24849–7

LIBRARY OF CONGRESS CATALOG CARD NO. 69–18649

BOOK DESIGN BY
DOROTHY ALDEN SMITH

Published by The Westminster Press ®
Philadelphia, Pennsylvania

PRINTED IN THE UNITED STATES OF AMERICA

"As Moses lifted up the serpent in the wilderness,
   so must the Son of Man be lifted up,
   that everyone who believes
   may in him have eternal life."

"When you have lifted up the Son of Man,
   then you will know who I am."

"Now is the judgment of this world,
   now shall the prince of this world
   be cast down;
   and I, when I am lifted up from the earth,
   will draw all men to myself."

CONTENTS

9

PRELIMINARY NOTE

"That which was from the beginning,
which we have heard,
which we have seen with our eyes,
which we have looked upon with our eyes,
which we have touched with our hands,
concerning the Word of life . . .

. . . .

we proclaim also to you,
so that you may have fellowship with us.
And as for our communion,
it is with the Father
and with his Son Jesus Christ.
All this we are writing to you
so that our joy may be complete."

These are the words of "the Elder," at the end of the
first century.

The church is the church to the extent that she believes and lives this testimony; to the extent that she
partakes of the faith of the apostles.

She has no other standard, no other foundation.

11

She is calling us to communion with her.
Communion of faith.
Communion of joy.

But it is impossible for this joy to be complete as long as the whole world is not sharing in it.

They "saw" and "touched."
We can only "see" and "touch" by faith. But the Lord's voice is still ringing out in those who hear his word and obey.
Now the apostle John invites us to listen and to contemplate.

The following notes are but a way of listening and contemplating.

The apostle John writes like Rembrandt paints: all is contrast of shadow and light.
Jesus is in the center, standing in an orb of light.
All the faces turned toward him are lighted up. Those who turn from him are in darkness.

Believing in the Son is passing from darkness to light, from death to life.
That is why all is submitted to him. Just as he is altogether submitted to his Father.
He is the divine Word made flesh.
His work is to establish the new form of worship, in spirit and in truth:
the new temple—his body;
the new baptism—baptism of water and of the Spirit;
the new Passover—his flesh and his blood given for the life of the world.

He is the nourishing Bread, the thirst-quenching Water, the life-giving Wine.

Heavenly liturgy, made incarnate. Transfigured matter, infused with life by the Spirit. An earnest of eternity.[3]

The incarnation is a breaking forth of eternity in time and space. With John we never cease passing from one level to the other—from the vision of the incarnate Son to the vision of the eternal Son in his Father's breast.

Everything that happens, every miracle, must be termed a *sign*. But Jesus' questioners only see the material part of the sign and not the reality meant to shine through. Hence the constant misunderstandings, John's way of expressing the Messianic secret. Jesus declares openly who he is, but only faith can understand the meaning of his words.[4]

This is how the discussion unfolds in the book of John. A far cry from the short incisive words of the Jesus we find in the Synoptic Gospels. John's style is more like a musical theme, taken up over and over again, elaborated, amplified.

What the beloved disciple—unknown, never giving his name—has heard, seen, contemplated, he hands down to us in his own language. The dialogue becomes a monologue, polemics becomes meditation.[1]

And now, unrelentingly, the darkness thickens, darkness which will only be pierced by the Easter brightness.

For John there is only one truly decisive *hour* in the world's history: when the only Son of the Father is lifted up on the cross of Calvary. Ultimate victory, ultimate defeat for the "prince of this world."

Mystery of a love stronger than all the powers of death.

The entire Gospel reaches out toward this singular hour, announces it, prepares its coming. For the salvation of the world depends on it.

Its concern, from beginning to end, is the case that God is bringing against men. And the case that men are bringing against God.

And the double judgment is handed down from the cross.[5]

The prosecution enters, the inquiry is opened.

Only one question is asked, and it dominates the proceedings: WHO IS THIS JESUS?—Son of God or impostor?

The case was entered in about A.D. 30. It is proceeding yet. It will go on till the end of time. For that inquiry contained the real question asked of all men, the only question that counts. If God really came, if he took on our human condition, if in our name he overcame all the powers of death, if he freed us from them, then the history of the world is forever changed, it takes on a final meaning.

If it is all an illusion, life is still only a race toward death.

And John is writing with this in mind. Fifty or sixty years have gone by since the Event. The church has forever broken away from the synagogue. And the whole debate turns on this one question: Is Jesus the awaited Messiah or is he not? Is he *more* than that?

Over against all the lights, all the wisdoms, all the speculations of his time, the author of the Fourth Gospel

14

opposes this unique Light, this unique Wisdom, this unique Glory of a God crucified for the salvation of men.

The unshakable opponents are "the Jews." This rather simplified outlook must be put back in its historical context. It must also be noticed that the Gospel makes a very clear distinction between the people and their leaders. But it is no less true that the most "religious" persons of that time, those who had been entrusted with the Law and the Old Testament promises were the ones who were immediately responsible for the crucifixion. And this is pregnant with meaning. The decisive battles are always fought at the very nerve center of the chosen people; that is where the real hand-to-hand combat between Satan and the Holy Spirit is taking place.

In the midst of the supping disciples there is a Judas. The church will have her saints, her lukewarm, her apostates.

Mystery of grace. Mystery of refusal.

John does not explain this double mystery. He simply invites us to the obedience of faith: **"These things are written that you may believe that Jesus is the Christ, the Son of God, and that believing you may have life in his name."**

PROLOGUE
John 1:1–18

Jesus Christ is the unique Word,[2b] the eternal Word, that God spoke to the world. This is why no other was spoken from the beginning and no other will be spoken until the end.

He is God's loving and merciful face turned toward this world. If that face were to turn away the slightest instant, the world would die, frozen in loneliness and terror, like an earth without a sun. For this light from God is the life of the world.

And thus humanity has life by the world-turned Face of Jesus Christ. In him God is looking at man, earnestly calling out to him, waiting for him. But man knows nothing of this.

This Face enlightens every man coming into the world, for without it he could neither be nor go on being. But man knows nothing of this.

When God reveals his presence to man, the hour of decision begins to strike. The hour of decision between darkness and light, between death and life.[7]

The Gospel proclaims to us that this hour has struck.

17

The Word of God once separated darkness from light and the world was born. He has come a second time to pierce the infinitely deeper darkness of sin and death. Men judge themselves by turning toward the light or by "preferring" the darkness.

The Lord will separate light from darkness a third time, at the day of his coming. Then will sin and death be swallowed up. All will see his face and night will be no more.

"The light shines in the darkness, and the darkness has never received it."

"The light shines in the darkness, and the darkness has never touched it" (or **"conquered it"**).

Two translations possible. The Western Church has long favored the first, the Eastern Church the second.*

The darkness of crucifixion day.

The Light of Easter morning.

"There was a man sent of God."

John the Baptist—the first witness of the trial about to begin: trial between God and his people; between God and humanity.

Herald of him whose coming is Light and Judgment.

Only a herald.

There are many lights in the world, many forms of wisdom clamoring for man's support. Over against all these lights, all these wisdoms, John sets **"the true light,"** the only one capable of shedding light on man's ultimate destiny.

Tragedy of ignorance, tragedy of refusal.

"The world knew him not."

"He came unto his own, and his own received him not."

18

Opaqueness of the world to God's light.

The Son comes into his own, the rightful heir to a world whose existence and meaning are in him only. But he goes unrecognized.

He comes "**unto his own**"—the people of the promise, the chosen people—and this people crucifies him.

"But to all who received him . . ."
The miracle of grace.

Of that new birth which, in and by Christ, makes of us sons and daughters of God.

Just as the eternal Son was begotten of the Holy Spirit in a body of flesh, so our carnal beings must be born of the Spirit unto life eternal.

Mystery of God's will unfolded in history, the only goal being that we might someday reflect his love and glory.

"The Word was made flesh."
The incarnation: a God who becomes man to save men;
   to walk beside them along life's roads,
   to share their hunger, their thirst, their weariness,
   to carry their burden of misery and shame,
   to die their death and give them life.

Jesus Christ, truly God and truly man; living the narrowly confined life of a Palestinian Jew; in an occupied country; under Pontius Pilate and Tiberius. Nevertheless sure of his unique destiny; knowing that his coming will change the face of the world.

   Lord, how difficult is it to believe it all?
   Both the grandeur and the abasement.

19

The folly of God, causing our Jewish and Moslem
brothers to cry blasphemy?

Listen! the apostolic church is here, standing and testi-
fying:
   **"He dwelt among us, full of grace and truth,
   and we beheld his glory."**
She is the one who **"knows."**
She has tasted of the new wine, she has drunk from the
cup of life.
She has contemplated the Lord in his double and
unique lifting up,
   on the cross, in the glory of his resurrection.
She knows that in him all is grace.
She knows that he is the truth of God.
And the truth of man.

**"From his fullness have we all received, grace upon
grace."**
   Fullness of the gift. Fullness of joy. Fullness of life.
   We are bidden to enter into this fullness.
   To enter in today—now.
   New dimensions of being of which we scarcely have an
inkling.
   A long road whose secret is held by God.

Moses and Jesus Christ: law and grace.
The Law announcing, preparing the reign of grace.
All revelation, incarnate in one life.
All man's grandeur, all his misery, laid bare.
His nothingness. His infinite possibilities.
The creative grace of life.
Of the fresh, new life which John calls:
ETERNAL LIFE.

"No one has ever seen God."

God, the holy, fearful One:

He whose glory human beings—even be it Moses—cannot see without dying.

God:

"The blessed and only Sovereign,
  the King of Kings and Lord of Lords,
  who alone has immortality
  and dwells in unapproachable light,
  whom no man has ever seen or can see." (I Tim.
6:15–16.)

This God, in Jesus Christ, takes on the veil of flesh,
So that through the Son we may know the Father.
And so that we may look on his Face without dying,
so that his holiness may not consume us,
his Son is the one who will die.

FIRST ENCOUNTERS
John 1:19–51

THE FIRST WITNESS

The case brought against God by the world, and that of God against the world unfolds from one end of the Gospel to the other. A trial during which Jesus now appears as the accused, now as the accuser, and now as the judge.

This trial must have witnesses.

John is the first and is quoted more often than any other.

His earthly life had this one purpose: to bear witness to the light **"that all might believe through him."**

The author of the Fourth Gospel is not interested in the historical John the Baptist, the man dressed in garments of camel's hair whose diet consisted of desert locusts, the prophet put to death for mincing no words with King Herod. His intention is to show that John was only the precursor, a voice proclaiming the coming of the Lord. Perhaps we have here an echo of more recent controversies between John's disciples and the Lord's.

Be that as it may, John appears to us as the most authentic type of witness: his greatness consists entirely in his voluntary self-effacement before him whose coming is imminent. He is nothing in himself, nothing but the watchman announcing the coming of the morning.

I am not the Messiah.

I am not Elijah.

I am not the expected "prophet."

I am a voice,

a voice crying in the wilderness:

"Make straight the way of the Lord."

The herald clearing the way for the King.

Is there anything greater?

Leonardo da Vinci's John the Baptist: one finger raised, larger than normal; in such a way that the only lasting impression is of the finger, pointed to heaven.

The witness' role is, always and only, to be that finger.

"Among you stands one whom you do not know."

"I myself did not know him either."

Here John puts all the emphasis on the verb "to know."

To know a person, to penetrate the mystery of his being: a much greater gift than we may think. For in that action must be committed one's whole being, there must be a mutual giving—there must be love.[8]

Mystery of Jesus Christ, impervious to the human eye. Only the Father knows it, only he reveals it.

And behold, John's eyes have been opened. From now on his entire ministry is meaningful only in this Greater-than-him, before whom self-effacement is a privilege and a joy.

The joy of the servant who wants to be unprofitable, forgotten, if only the king enters in, is believed and acclaimed.

The joy of the bridegroom's friend who has only one thought: the consummation of the royal wedding.

"Behold the Lamb who takes away the sins of the world." [2d]

The lamb: symbol of sacrificed life, of deliverance and of offering.

Blood of the lamb which saved the Israelites from death.

Paschal lamb offered and eaten every year on the fourteenth day of Nisan.

The Servant of Isaiah, a lamb dumb before its shearers.

From the very beginning of time the offering was prepared, proclaimed, pointed out.

And now the hour has come when it must become reality.

When baptism will no longer be of water and repentance only, but of blood and of Spirit;

and it will give life.

THE FIRST DISCIPLES

John is not in the least surprised that his disciples should leave him to follow Jesus; that is the proper order established by God.

"Rabbi—where are you staying?—Come and see."

The simplicity of this first encounter. The time is given very precisely as four o'clock in the afternoon,

24

and it is added that they stayed until the evening. Oh, how we would like to know about this first encounter! Nothing is said of it.

The modesty of these meetings where destinies are decided. It is better they be known only of God.

But every real encounter becomes a mission. Andrew brings his brother Simon back to Jesus.

Jesus *looks at* Simon.

The decisive moment is not when we look at Jesus but when *he* looks at us.

"You are Simon the son of John, you will be called Cephas"—that is Peter.

A destiny has been decided in that single look, that single word.

Simon will be the "rock" on which the Lord will build his church.

It will be a long road for you, Simon. You're ardent. You're versatile. But what difference can it make: your name is written in heaven. The Lord knows of what you are made. He has chosen you. That's enough.

Jesus calls Philip. One brief order: "Follow me."

Follow me and you will know who I am.

And Philip calls Nathanael. Chain reaction: each disciple attracts another.

The Israelite without guile confesses his doubt, Can anything good come out of Nazareth?—Philip does not argue with him: **"Come and see."**

Anything else we say is usually superfluous. Jesus must be *shown*.

Amazement. The faith is here to discover oneself as seen, known, loved, from all eternity.

25

"Truly, truly, I say to you, you will see heaven opened and the angels of God ascending and descending upon the Son of Man." [2a]

Jacob's dream become reality. The Son, living bridge between heaven and earth.

Blessed and fearful presence:

"The Lord is in this place and I did not know it." (Gen. 28:16.)

TWO SIGNS OF THE NEW ERA
John, Ch. 2

CANA

Mother, what are you asking of me?
My hour is not yet come.[6]
The hour of the blood-filled wedding, of the eternal wedding,
  when my blood will flow like generous wine.

The jars for purification rites. The free wine flowing strong like a river:
  two dispensations;
  two covenants;
  two baptisms,
Lustral water changed into wine for the Supper.

The church's Husband participating in this village wedding blesses the human couple and their earthly joy with a simple act; in his eyes their joy is healthy and legitimate.
Human love sanctified, transfigured by the divine Presence.

27

"Husbands, love your wives as Christ loved the church and gave himself up for her." (Eph. 5:25.) New wine poured into old wineskins.

"He manifested his glory, and his disciples believed in him." For the others the sign is no less obscure.

THE TEMPLE

Lord, I love you, whip in hand, angry with a holy anger, driving merchants and money changers out of your Father's house.

What do you think, Lord, of our holy gatherings,
so sober, so pious, sometimes so glum?

But of course, we no longer buy and sell in your sanctuaries,
that is work for the week.

And we bring you a solemn, reassuring offering,
the miserly hundreth of our profits.

The tabernacle, place of the ineffable Presence,
the Holy of Holies which is entered once a year, with trembling,
and this construction which took forty-six years,
is all this nothing in your eyes?

Soon now the bells will ring out the hour of the new worship service.

The hour when men will worship in spirit and in truth.[6]

Henceforth the place of the Presence,
the place where God is glorified,
will be the body of a man, of a crucified man.

The body of the resurrected Man.

Body of Christ. Body of the church. Temple of flesh.

28

Dim and hidden glory.

So hidden that the disciples will only grasp the Lord's words much later;

when all is finished.

"The Lord has said that he would dwell in thick darkness." (I Kings 8:12.)

Secret of the old tabernacle.

Secret of a humble life as a Palestinian Jew.

Secret of his presence in the bread and wine.

Secret of his presence in his body—which is the church.

"Many believed."

Jesus, no one to cherish illusions, **for "he himself knew what was in man."**

ENTRY INTO THE KINGDOM
John, Ch. 3

NICODEMUS

Factual details readily take on symbolic worth in the Gospel of John. Nicodemus comes to find Jesus "by night." It is "night" when Judas leaves the upper room to plunge into the darkness of betrayal and death.

Nicodemus comes to Jesus: for a moment he comes into the orb of light. Then he disappears as he came. The night closes up on him again.

This man personifies the party of the Pharisees in its most open attitude:

"Rabbi, we know that you are a teacher come from God; no one can do these signs that you do, unless God is with him."

Would it not seem that the dialogue has got off to a good start? a rabbi-to-rabbi, theologian-to-theologian dialogue. Will Jesus encourage such an example of goodwill?—No. Jesus reins him up abruptly.

"Nicodemus, we aren't here to talk about me and my miracles. We're here to talk about *your* new birth, *your* entry into the Kingdom."

30

—"How can a man be born when he is old?"

An apparently absurd misunderstanding. In fact, two worlds are facing each other, and they have no common language. A "down here" world, and an "up there" world, letter and spirit, carnal realities and eternal realities.

To make the passage from one world to the other, nothing less will suffice than a "new birth."

—"You are a teacher in Israel, and you do not know these things?"

You do not believe in this renewing of all things announced by the Scriptures?

You do not believe that the Spirit has the power to change our lives?

—Lord, I am no different from Nicodemus: "Can the Ethiopian change his skin or the leopard his spots?" (Jer. 13:23.) Will I ever break with all my past life? Lord, I know myself too well!

Nicodemus has left. The dialogue has failed. And yet, the memory of this night will not escape him. One day soon, before the Sanhedrin, he will defend Jesus (John 7:48–50). And for his sepulcher he will bring one hundred pounds of incense (John 19:39).

The tragedy of one who has a presentiment of truth, but backs off from a committal of self (John 12:42).

THE SON OF MAN IS LIFTED UP [2a]

The mystery of baptism:
unavoidably linked to the incarnation;
to the Son's coming down among men;

to his death, to his resurrection;
to his ascension;
to the gift of the Spirit.

Miracle of grace, miracle of forgiveness.
Virgin birth, and God breathes his spirit over all.
The coming of the Word: **"To all who received him,
he gave power to become children of God,
to those who believe in his name,
who were born,
not of blood nor of the will of the flesh,
nor of the will of man,
but of God."**
Mystery of this breath from above—coming from
no one knows where,
nor does anyone know where it will take us.
Wind from the summits.
Wind of freedom
sweeping away the miasmas of earth.
A new, steady look at things.
Believe the efficacy of my baptism:
the mystery of pardon, of grace, and of life,
a new beginning—always possible—
of which it is the surety.
Believe the power of the Spirit
who tears me away from myself
and "christifies" me.

I am not mistaken, Lord, that *is* what you want,
isn't it?
to re-create us in your image, after your likeness,
to pour into us your love and your life?
That is why you came,
why you came down,

why you went up,
why you conquered.

The apostles believed: **"We know and bear witness
to what we have seen."**
What is earthly, they tell us, does not know the
heavenly.
And it is not a question of setting the temporal and
the spiritual over against each other, but rather a short
and a long way of looking at things: shortsightedness
stops at the sign, but farsightedness grasps its meaning.
Grasp the reality underneath the symbol, the eternal
in the instant.
And in everything, where it will finally lead to.

**"As Moses lifted up the serpent in the wilderness,
so must the Son of Man be lifted up,[2a]
that everyone who believes
may in him have eternal life."** [7]

A rather strange story—that of the bronze serpent
that we are told Moses set up in the desert by an order
from God, to save the Israelites from death:
"Whoever is bitten, when he looks upon it, shall live"
(Num. 21:8).

**"He who looked toward it was not saved because he
was contemplating it,
but by you, universal Savior."**

. . . .

**"Your mercy helped them in their need and saved
them. . . .
It is neither herbs nor ointment that saved them,
but thy word, Lord, healed all."** (Wisd. of Sol. 16:7,
10,12.)

And this all-powerful word comes down from the
cross.

The baleful power nailed to the cross, reduced to
powerlessness.

Jesus nails it there by dying.

Contemplation of the Son on the cross—power of
salvation and of life.

He must be looked upon,
until his own eye rests on us,
and penetrates as the sun itself unto our prides,
our self-sufficiencies,
our bitterness, and our rebelliousness,
and nails them to the wood
of *his* cross.

Then the mystery of infinite mercy
opens to our wondering eyes.

GRACE AND JUDGMENT

**"Yes, God so loved the world
that he gave his only Son[2c]
so that whoever believes in him
should not perish
but have eternal life."**

God loved *the world.*

Lord, how strange your love is.

You let us wander on any and every road.

Roads of lies, of hate and of death.

You let the innocent one die, and the guilty one
triumph.

You let entire races be assassinated.

You let injustice triumph.

And you let the prince of this world knock you around.

When at last you break the silence
and you send us your Son, your only Son,[2e]
it is for him to suffer and die,
—on a cross.

Lord, you ask me to believe
that my salvation cost this much?

That outside the sovereign gift of this life,
the world would perish?

—Yes, my child, for living is loving.

The secret of life is in the given life.

And only infinite love
can make the spark of life break forth in a man's
existence.

I can do anything—anything except force men to love me: all I can do, up here nailed to the cross, is to invite them.

From the beginning of time, that is where I have been waiting for you—for all of you men.

**"God sent his Son into the world,
not to condemn the world,
but that the world through him might be saved."**

Grace always precedes judgment.

God leaves it up to men to judge themselves, by opening up to light, or by refusing it.

That is where our liberty is decided.

**"And this is the judgment:
the light has come into the world,**

**and men loved darkness rather than light,
because their deeds were evil."** [7]
The devil's sport is to make us enjoy our chains.

Adam fled: and since that first flight, man's instinct
is to hide:
from God;
from others;
and from self.
Fear that our works will be brought to light—not so
much our evil works as those reputed to be good.
Dread of being unmasked.
All these fears will fasten the Just One's cross in place.
But this cross, the very same cross, is what unmasks us,
unavoidably.
And it will save us by unmasking us.

"But he who 'does the truth' [10]
**comes to the light,
that it may be clearly seen
that his deeds have been wrought in God."**
Practice the truth: faithfulness to the glimpsed light,
no matter how limited it may be. On this faithfulness
will depend any progress toward the light.
Lord, in this faithfulness to perceived light, I im-
agine many unbelievers are ahead of us; and they are
moving toward you without being aware of it.
But how will it be with those who, purposely, turn
away from what they know to be *true,* whatever kind of
truth it may be? May it be that they will lose even the
capability of seeing?
Voluntary blindness.
That can become mortal.

36

JOHN BEARS WITNESS AGAIN

The Fourth Gospel is the only one to mention Jesus and John working in Judea at the same time. Their disciples baptize and rivalry is the result.

The apostolic church knew a baptism of John as distinct from that of Jesus (Acts 18:25; 19:1–5). And that is why John emphasizes the point, in reminding us, a second time, that John testified himself for the Lord and voluntarily humbled himself before him.

The joy of the Bridegroom's friend who stands near and listens.

The greatness of this person contemplating from afar, by faith, the wedding feast of the church.

Standing, like Moses, on the threshold of the Promised Land.

John the Baptist, earthly figure—but the greatest because of his finger pointing toward that perfect joy which is his.

Oh, to be one of those who always make the questioner look beyond them,

toward the only One worthy of being looked upon.

SAVIOR OF THE WORLD
John, Ch. 4

JESUS IN SAMARIA

Traveling through Samaria, Jesus stops a while. This story is related only in the Fourth Gospel.

Samaria: a country most hostile to Jews (Luke 9:51–56). For the Jews an apostate country, radically impure, syncretistic in religion, and therefore worse than heathen. The conflict goes back more than six hundred years to the Assyrian invasion. (See II Kings 17:5–6, 24–41; Ezra 4:1–10.)

Intentional contrast: John has arranged the order so that after the dialogue with Nicodemus the Pharisee comes the dialogue with the Samaritan woman and the conversion of the Samaritans. Firstfruits of future harvests. (Acts 8:4–8.) It is the Samaritans who will recognize in Jesus "the Savior of the world."

The discussion takes place "at Jacob's well," on this bit of ground once given by Jacob to his son Joseph[9] (Josh. 24:32; Deut. 33:28). From the Jewish canon the Samaritans have kept only the Pentateuch. They are proud of their forefathers' traditions, proud of their sacred wells. Is water not the symbol of the law—purify-
38

ing, thirst-quenching, life-giving?

Well of Tradition. Living water of the new dispensation. Once again the dawning of Messianic times is announced.

"Give me a drink."

A self-respecting Jew does not speak with a woman.

A Jew does not ask a Samaritan woman for a drink.

All the world's ostracisms, all the taboos, all the "apartheids," challenged with this one act. With this one drink of water.

Jesus *asks*, he who can give all. Thus the conversation starts on an equal footing. Is a certain mutualness not the condition of all true dialogue?

But here again the discussion unfolds on two different levels. The words of one are spirit and life, those of the other are still clinging to material, everyday reality.

"Are you greater than our father Jacob?" The Jacob who, according to the legend, made the water rise up to the lip of the well?

—Woman, don't you know that when the Messiah comes a stream will flow from the sanctuary, resurrecting life where death reigned before? Don't you know that, according to the prophets' predictions, the desert will blossom like a rose? And that even your soul, empty of joy, will burst into bloom? (Isa. 35:1–7; Ezek. 47:1–12; Rev. 22:1–2.)

—No, she knows nothing of all this. How could she know?

All this has no meaning except in faith. And she is not possessor of this faith.

"Go call your husband and come back here."

The existential question has now been asked, the

secret of this life has been unveiled. Above and beyond this woman is it not the destiny of Samaria which is in view, this Samaria whose unfaithfulness she symbolizes?

The woman acknowledges her fault:

"Lord, I see that you are a prophet."

You are a prophet, you know the hidden things. In that case, tell me where I should be worshiping. On Gerizim or at Jerusalem? . . . Where is the true God?

The answer falls, categorically, in two parts:

"Salvation is from the Jews."

The axis of revelation runs through Israel. And nowhere else.

"But the hour is coming—and already is—when the true worshipers will worship the Father in spirit and in truth."

A double statement forever linking the two Testaments, the prediction and the fulfillment.

"Salvation comes from the Jews."

It is to them that the Living God, **"I AM,"** revealed himself.

It is to them that the sacred trust of faith was committed.

The Messiah was announced to them. His coming prepared by them.

It was with Jewish flesh that God became incarnate.

Salvation comes from the Jews: a statement that unappeasably condemns all the anti-Semitisms of all time.

"God is Spirit."

Gerizim, Jerusalem, places forever transcended
by the new worship in spirit and in truth.
All temples of stone rendered profane
by the coming of the incarnate Word.

Jars for purification and new wine.
Temple of stone and temple of flesh.
Baptism of water and baptism of the Spirit.
Jacob's well and springing water.

The Messianic era has been ushered in.

"I know that the Messiah is to come."
The Samaritans as well as the Jews are waiting for the Messiah. This woman is also waiting for his coming.
Then the decisive word is pronounced: **"I AM (he)."**
The sacred Tetragrammaton spoken on Sinai.

The greatest mystery of faith announced not to the disciples but to this foreigner.

The woman in her excitement forgets her water jar, and runs to the village to tell of her encounter: hardly a proselyte and already a missionary.
"Come and see a man who told me all that I ever did. Is this not the Christ?"
Her heart burns within her. She cannot keep silent. She must lead the others to this extraordinary man who, perhaps, is the Messiah . . .

THE TIME OF HARVEST

The disciples are back with the provisions. They are dumbfounded to find their Master conversing with this woman. But they would not dare to question him. And the misunderstanding of a moment ago is about to be reproduced. This time it is not about water, but about food. The disciples, like the woman, like Nicodemus,

41

live and move only on the level of material realities. The words of Jesus are spirit and life. Because their words do not have the same meaning, misunderstanding results.

A language problem?—Yes, probably. But it must be added that beneath this problem there is another, much more profound. And that the real divergence turns on the meaning and the goal of existence.

Thus Jesus' words will always be, for the disciples as for all others, puzzling, enigmatic, until the resurrection; then only will their eyes open to the realities of faith, that for the present they can only vaguely feel.

But, to the extent of their present attainments, they listen to the Master and follow him. And that is what is asked of them.

"My food is to do the will of my Father and to accomplish his work."

This work is the salvation of the world. The Father and the Son united in this same will, in this same combat. But the Son in all submitted to the Father. "Nourished" by him at every hour. Giving only what he has received beforehand.

"Lift up your eyes and see how the fields are already white for the harvest."

There are four months from sowing time to harvesttime. But here we have sowing and reaping coinciding.

The woman who has just left, the men who are going to leave,
these half heathen, these Samaritans,
are the firstfruits of the harvest of the world.
Already, by faith, I see the ripe heads of grain.
I see the reapers' sickles.

42

Gathering the sheaves that Another has sown,
putting the harvest into the bins of my Father's
granaries.

The sower's joy, the reaper's joy.
The Son's joy, the Father's joy.
The joy of the workers of the first hour and of the
eleventh hour.
Who would not wish to participate in such a work?

The Samaritans have come.
They have invited to their village this unknown Jew.
They have listened—believed:
**"We have heard for ourselves, and we know that this
is indeed the Savior of the world."**

RETURN TO CANA: A HEALING

"Your son lives."
The Samaritans *took Jesus' word,* without the need
for miracles.
The Galileans go to him because of his miracles:
"Because of all he did in Jerusalem."
The king's official, for his part, struggles for his son's
life. And knows that Jesus has the power to heal him.
And *believes* his word.
Second miracle in Cana: he who has the power to
change water into wine has the power to restore life.
All-powerfulness of the *Word,* which is *Life.*

THE SON'S WORK: TO GIVE LIFE
John, Ch. 5

THE HEALING OF THE PARALYTIC

In the Gospel of John we see Jesus going regularly up to Jerusalem for the ritual feasts.

It is at Jerusalem that all the controversies with the Jewish authorities take place, and that, from one event to another, the tragedy of rejection comes to a head. Jerusalem, the only fatherland of every Israelite.

Jerusalem who kills the prophets.

Jerusalem, most favored spot on earth, where the Son must fight the supreme battle to bring his people back to belief.

The pool of Bethesda: veritable concentration of the world's maladies.

A man is there, he has not left his bed for thirty-eight years.

The Lord looks at him: **"Do you want to be healed?"**

"Lord, I have no one." No one who shares my infirmity. No one who enters into the loneliness of my suffering and of my pain.

He is looking at you, at you and at no one else.

44

Even today, you who "have no one," you can be sure that he sees you.

Pain of body, pain of soul. Secret pain that no one knows.

He *knows*.

And this pain—if he does not heal it, he bears it with you.

The man is walking, he is healed. He knows not by whom.

Jesus, still today, is walking anonymously among men. He does many things, but we will know only at the Last Day that *it was he*.

Jesus meets the man a second time and warns him: **"Sin no more, that nothing worse befall you."**

Every grace: a greater responsibility.

Every healing accomplished by Jesus is a victory won over the prince of death, a sign—a forerunner—of the Reign:

"Then the eyes of the blind shall be opened, and the ears of the deaf unstopped. Then shall the lame man leap like a hart, and the tongue of the dumb sing for joy. Waters shall break forth in the wilderness, and streams in the desert." (Isa. 35:5–6.)

What joy is this man's, to find the use of his body again after *thirty-eight years!*

The religious authorities do not in the least share this joy: what is important is not that this man has been healed, but that everything should proceed according to the rules. Who is this intruder who thinks himself up to doing miracles?

And who is breaking the law. That man was healed on a Sabbath Day!

Even more: he was ordered to carry his bed. Is it not written: **"Take heed for the sake of your lives not to bear a burden on the Sabbath Day"?** (Jer. 17:21–22.)

What right has Jesus to do these things?

And Jesus answers: by my Son's rights.

For those who do not believe in his Messiahship, a frightful blasphemy.

We must grasp the depth of the problem as stated in those terms. The controversy henceforth is to rage around Jesus himself.

Son of God or blasphemer: there is no middle ground.

When John is writing his Gospel the situation between Christians and Jews can be summed up in that question. And the same question is still being asked of every human conscience.

And according to whether it is settled or not Christianity will be truth or delusion.

For some, blasphemy.

THE SON'S WORK IS THE FATHER'S WORK

"My Father is working still, and I am working."

United work of Father and Son stretching from the beginning to the end of time.

Mysterious gestation.

It took millions of years before a man was made.

And before man knew he was called of God.

Before he was born to eternal life.

"Truly, truly, I say to you,
The Son can do nothing of his own accord."
Total, joyous subordination of the Son to the Father.
But perfect identity of will, of the goal in mind.
Work of the Son, integral and faithful reflection of
the Father's work.
Work so great, that even today his disciples cannot
measure its breadth,
and they will marvel at it throughout eternity.

The Father loves the Son and has put everything under
his power:
the judgment of the world,
the power of giving life.[7]
Whoever believes in the Son escapes the judgment:
"He has passed from death to life."
Power is given to the Son to resurrect the "dead" that
we are; to make them be born again today—now—unto
eternal life.
Thus, what we call the "land of the living" is often
made up only of walking dead men.
The voice of the Son—alone empowered to open the
sepulchers of the world.

The Son, sovereign Judge and all-powerful liberator,
for he knows of what man is made.
The Son, only standard for what we call "good" or
"evil";
for he is "Man" in his divine and human fullness.

To be made like the Son, eternal Image of the invisible
God, such is the only goal, the only meaning of all
human life.

47

THE WITNESSES

According to Jewish law, any condemnation requires that two or three witnesses be heard. It is only proper that the trial of the Son of God proceed according to the rules (Deut. 19:15).

John, the first witness: shining flame which, when the night is darkest, heralds the Morning.

You rejoiced in his light. You refused to receive his message.

Second testimony: that rendered to the Son by the Father himself by the works that he has granted him to accomplish.

Every one of the Son's works is marked with the Father's seal. Any question referred to the Father.

Just as every one of our works should carry the Son's seal, referring to him only who accomplishes them.

Third testimony: that of the Scriptures.

Privileged people, unique people, to whom God *spoke*. Whose entire history is a dialogue with the Living God.

But also, by some strange mystery, a blind, deaf people, and it always has been;

a people that does not know the hour of its deliverance (Isa. 43:8–13).

A people that reads, examines, comments, endlessly the sacred text,

and does not grasp its full meaning.

But the ones who accuse you are the very ones you claim as your own:

Moses and the Prophets, all those who from age to age

have hoped for, believed in, and acclaimed My Day.

The skies have been torn apart, God has come down among you. But your eyes stay shut; because you are seeking, not his glory, but yours.

Lord, we also search your Scriptures. Have we grasped their promise of life?

Are we not, in turn, "blind and deaf"?

And this great Work of salvation which they spread out before our eyes—

are we really involved in it?

Lord, may we always remember,

that the science of the Scriptures, indulged in as an end in itself,

can kill the Word that it claims to be commenting.

And the sacred Book can become only a press-book of dried flowers,

learnedly cataloged.

Grant us anew your Word which is Life,

our calling, our judgment, your promise, the resurrection of the dead!

THE BREAD OF LIFE
John, Ch. 6

The Galilean ministry of Jesus is very briefly mentioned in the Fourth Gospel. It is assumed to be known.

If the miracle of the loaves and fishes is recounted, it is because this event has a particular meaning for John the Evangelist. He situates it at the time of the Jewish Passover. He is the only one to bring out its inner meaning: the material bread becomes the sign and symbol of another bread: the bread sent from heaven.

Eucharistic mystery. New Passover which is to nourish the world.

And thus, little by little, one stroke after another, John's theme of the new worshiping in spirit and truth is developed.

A new way of worshiping—the Lord is its temple, its offering, and its sacrificial lamb, giving his flesh for the renewing of the world.

A new communion whose visible signs are the baptism of water and of the Spirit, the wine and the bread.

But along with this liturgical initiation, as a tragic backdrop, unfolds a strand of incomprehension and rejection. Just as the sign given to the Jews at Jerusalem, the healing of the paralytic, has laid bare their unbelief, in the same way the sign given to the Galileans, after a fleeting enthusiasm, will lead to their withdrawal.

FIVE LOAVES AND TWO FISH

"What are they among so many?"
Philip and Andrew's reaction is that of realism and common sense.
It is also ours when we face the great hunger of men. What can I do! There are too many of them.
Gross common sense of those who "belong to this earth" and do not believe in the miracles of love and faith.
But scattered here and there around the world, there are a few, "crazy for God," who believe—and who prove it.
Why, Lord, are they so rare? Your world is so hungry. Hungry for love and hungry for bread.

"Jesus then took the loaves, and when he had given thanks, he distributed them to those who were seated, as much as they wanted; so also the fish."
Feeding of the five thousand, sign of God's fullness. Prelude to the great banquet at the end of time.
A meal, symbol of communion.
There are those with whom one eats. And those with whom one does not eat.
All ancient covenants were sealed with a meal.
Such was the case with Abram and Melchizedek who sealed their pact using the sign of bread and wine.
Hospitality offered to angels under the oak of Mamre. (Icon of the Trinity.)

51

The seventy elders, on Mt. Horeb, are described to us
as eating and drinking in God's presence.
(Seventy: the figure of the fullness of the nations.)
Israel in the desert: fed by God himself on manna
and water from the rock.

The end of time is seen by the prophets as an era of
plenty when men will at last have enough.
"They shall no longer hunger nor thirst
for he who has pity on them shall lead them,
and by springs of water will guide them." (Isa. 49:10.)

"Ho, everyone who thirsts, come to the waters;
and he who has no money, come,
buy grain and eat, without money,
and without price, wine and milk." (Isa. 55:1.)
Wisdom stands upright in the crossroads of the city.
The table is ready.
Ho, men! All you have to do is to enter.
"Come, eat of my bread
and drink of the wine I have mixed.
Leave folly behind, and you shall live,
Walk in the way of truth." (Prov. 9:5–6.)

Lord, this Messianic era so often announced—
Should the crowd be blamed for thinking it has
arrived?
Over and again, during the course of history,
false messiahs have cheated their hopes.
And now, in these most obvious signs
they recognize in you the prophet they have been
awaiting.

But you, aware of the crowd's wanting to make you
King,

you go away.
No, you are not King in their fashion.

And now you are alone on the mountain.
Have you fled the crowd—or temptation?
This crowd is so pitiful, it understands nothing
of your way of doing things,
of your delays.
Today, it wants to be filled.
Today, it wants to be liberated.
And not, Lord, at the end of time!
In this battle, as in all the others,
you are **"all alone."**
Alone with your Father.

IN THE BOAT

The disciples afraid on a furious sea,
afraid of the phantom suddenly appearing.
"It is I; do not be afraid."
Sometimes this is how you come to us, in the darkest
hours of our lives,
and you lay your reassuring hand on our shoulder:
"Do not be afraid; I am here."

TRUE LABOR

**"Labor not for the food which perishes, but for the
food which endures to eternal life."**
Jesus is not denying the necessity of working for a

53

living. Not at all. He knows what it means. This necessity is a part of God's plan: **"If anyone will not work, let him not eat"** (II Thess. 3:10).

Neither is it a question of setting some indefinable, high-flown spirituality over against material work.

But rather to discern the meaning, the utlimate goal, of every existence, and to classify everything according to this goal.

Empty of life, riveted to the earth. Absorbed by the humdrum of everyday life; or by business cares: by that game which attracts our interest, and ends up absorbing us altogether.

The tangy taste of profit.

Work—virtue and devil of the Western world.

—Yes, but what is **"working the works of God"**?

The rabbi might answer: Observance of the law, tithing, respect for the Sabbath;

the zealous Christian: Sunday school, choir, and deacon service?

We all want "to do something for God."

What about these words: **"This is the work of God, that you believe in him whom he has sent."**

Believe the Son of Man: believe his word, believe his promises, believe what he is and what he wants us to be.

Take him seriously.

Just as his food is to do the Father's will, so ours will be to do his will.

He who believes in him will do God's work as naturally as the tree bears its fruit.

54

THE TRUE BREAD FROM HEAVEN

The crowd asks for a sign: manna falling anew from heaven.

He who gives this manna is standing before them, but they know it not.

Here now is someone greater than Moses, greater than the miracles of the desert.

They were only figures and signs of Him who was to come.

You murmured then. You murmur now.

You always murmur.

But he whom the Father draws, and who believes,
he who comes to Me,
will be forever nourished and filled
at the great banquet of life.

And *I will resurrect him at the Last Day.*

(This promise is repeated three times.)

And "the Jews" begin murmuring again: How can this man say that he has come down from heaven? . . . We know his father and mother!

Jesus' origins, permanent subject of controversy.

And they always will be.

Only the Son reveals the Father. But the Father, also, is the only one who reveals the Son, **"draws"** all men to him.

Paradox of faith with which all our human logic locks horns.

For the Gospel tells us just as firmly that only those may believe to whom it has been granted, as that the Jews are guilty of their unbelief.

Only faith can grasp the two opposing terms because it lives the truth they represent.

It knows that grace is everything. It knows that in the order of faith, God is always first, bringing forth amens from our rebellious lips.

But it also knows the fearful liberty to refuse that God has left us, and all the ways we have of resisting his coming.

Its amazement never ceases before the mystery of grace always renewed, always unmerited.

> **"I am the Bread of Life**
> **come down from heaven.**
> **Whoever shall eat of this bread**
> **will live eternally.**
> **And the bread that I shall give**
> **for the life of the world is my flesh."**

Living bread of the Word which must be received, assimilated, must become within us vital energy, as material bread becomes blood, flesh, and muscle. Continuous re-creation of our being by this Word which is Spirit and life.

> This Word was made flesh
> and this flesh is given for the life of the world.
> Living bread, eucharistic bread.

> **"Whoever eats my flesh**
> **and drinks my blood**
> **abides in me**
> **and I in him."**

> Nurtured by his given life,
> by his resurrected body.
> United by faith to this life, to this resurrection,
> in the most vital union which is capable of being.

"Whoever will eat this bread will live forever."
The greatest mystery of faith:
Presence real but hidden
by the materialness of the species,
to vivify our whole being,
body, soul, and spirit
and to be the promise
of our eternity.

Inseparable unity of the sign and of the word,
one conferring on the other its reality,
for only the Word, being spirit and life,
communicates its everlastingness to the flesh.

Mystery of the Son, who once in history
became flesh with our very flesh
who once in history shed his blood
to unite us in him, inseparably,
nourished from one flesh, vivified by one
blood.

Eucharist! Thanksgiving and praise
for whoever believes.
For anyone else,
Scandal and blasphemy.

Sacramental realism of the first Christians,
stumbling block for Jews and heathen.
Jesus accused of a kind of anthropophagy.
"This is a hard saying; who can listen to it?"

**"After this many of his disciples drew back and no
longer went about with him."**
King of the Jews, he would have had a following.

Prophet, he would perhaps have been listened to.

But Son of Man come down from heaven, Son of Man giving us his flesh to eat,

declaring himself to be the only guarantor of our eternity?

PETER'S CONFESSION

Here we find the breaking point between unbelief and faith.

There is no longer any middle ground. The hour to choose has struck.

"Will you also go away?"

—"Lord, to whom would we go? You have the words of eternal life."
Simon Peter speaking.
The church's confession of faith throughout all ages.

"We believe" . . . **"we know."** [8]
Certainty lived out.
From age to age your Word has quickened our life,
your Sacraments have nurtured and consoled us,
unfaithful servants, overwhelmed with your goodness.
But to the very heart of the Cenacle
the demon has crept.

A SIGN OF CONTRADICTION
AMONG MEN
John, Ch. 7

THE FEAST OF TABERNACLES

According to the apostle John, the trial of the Son of Man unfolds entirely at Jerusalem.

For that reason the periods spent in Galilee are only forced interludes between any two trips to Jerusalem:

"He could not move about in Judea, because the Jews were trying to kill him."

The Son of God wandering about as a fugitive in his own territory. Brother of all the fugitives of all time.

Every good Jew goes up to Jerusalem for the three great feasts of the year. And now the Feast of Tabernacles is almost upon us.

Joyous feast, feast of thanksgiving and of praise, feast of the harvest. Commemoration of the exodus, of the march through the desert, of the miracles of God. Expectation of the Great Day when the Messiah is to come. When streams of living water will flow from the sanctuary.

If Jesus is the Messiah, is it not time to prove it?

to rally around him all of Judea?

This is how Jesus' brothers reason with the reasonings of the flesh. **"For even his brothers did not believe in him."**

Pressure by the next of kin, half-ironical insinuations: you have been acquainted with all this, also, Lord. Biting loneliness, among your very own.

"My time has not yet come,[6] but your time is always here. The world cannot hate you, but it hates me because I testify of it that its works are evil."

"My time has not yet come . . ." The time will come, the determined hour, when he must make the last trip, amid the acclamations of a crowd ready to crown him king—and which tomorrow will abandon him.

The hour when the Son is lifted upon the cross.

"Your time is always here." Your pious gestures have no meaning; why should the world hate its like?

Your religion bothers no one.

Lord, have we also made your message so dull that it has lost its sting? Will the tolerance of the world, which we boast of, someday be our condemnation?

For the world is quite happy to leave us our "religion," as long as it does not try to put the world out of business.

And out of all the worlds, the religious world is the most fearful of being unmasked; and its hate will be the most relentless. That is why it kills the prophets and suspects the saints.

—It can always canonize them later on.

60

The people of Jerusalem are looking for Jesus and "whispering" about him; in every group he is the topic of conversation: **"He is a good man"**—**"No, he is leading the people astray."**

It is the middle of the feast when Jesus appears in the Temple and begins teaching: **"How does this man happen to be learned, he has never studied in our schools?"**

The Holy Spirit takes some strange liberties!

"If any man's will is to do God's will, he will know whether my doctrine is of God or whether I am speaking on my own authority." Obedience—the only sure road to knowledge: such a sure and simple criterion that we always look for another.

Take God at his word: believe his word and live from it.

The Son's authority is based on his perfect identity with his Father's will. Thus everything he says and does is only for God's glory.

Our human vainglory always wants to add its little stamp to God's work. And thus, while we are serving him, we are really looking out for our own glory.

"He who speaks on his own authority seeks his own glory; but he who seeks the glory of him who sent him is true, and in him there is no disloyalty."

That is a strong word. Every embezzlement for ourselves of a glory belonging only to God is a "disloyalty." But it is just as **"disloyal"** to present our human cogitations as coming from God.

Submissiveness to the Word, to the Holy Spirit its only interpreter, to his testimony throughout the centuries.

Submissiveness that always brings us back to the feet of Jesus.

That requires a lot of time, a lot of prayer, a lot of humble waiting.

We are in a hurry. And thus we hand out—to ourselves—as though it were coming straight from the Word, a great deal of counterfeit currency.

The Jews claimed Moses as theirs, we claim the gospel; but our very real unfaithfulness keeps us from making any progress in our search for truth.

"I did one deed, and you all marvel at it."

Probably a reference to the healing of the paralytic. The controversy takes up again where it left off (ch. 5:47). Jesus meets his adversaries on their own ground and proves to them by Moses that his action is legitimate.

Fairness requires that the true meaning of the accomplished act be ascertained as well as the authority backing it up.

But that would be recognizing that the Messianic era has arrived.

We are at the very heart of the conflict.

And now around the main speakers on every side the entire population is excitedly talking: **"Is this not the man 'they' are seeking to kill? And here he is speaking openly!"** . . . **"Can it be that 'they' have recognized him?"** But of course not! When the Messiah comes, no one will know whence he comes. **"But still . . ."**

The question of Jesus' origins is forever being asked afresh. The question of his human birth, of his divine nature.

Jesus known, yet not known. For he alone knows whence he has come and where he is going.

The tension mounts. The leaders among the priests

take counsel together: this has gone on long enough! There is too much whispering going around about him! He must be arrested! But his hour has not yet come. Jesus continues his preaching. Time is short, the hour of departure has almost arrived:

"You will seek me, and you will not find me."

Another round of misunderstandings: is he going to flee to the Greeks and begin teaching them, also?

For John this misunderstanding probably has a prophetic meaning. Yes, the day is coming when the Lord will visit the Greeks; for his field of action is the world. And those who have rejected his words will look for him, but will no longer be able to find him.

"Where I am
you cannot come."

Only faith can reach him where he will henceforth be: in the bosom of his Father.

Lord, is it possible that those who have thrown away their opportunities will never have another chance?

LIVING WATER

The last day of the feast has arrived.

The day when liturgy celebrates, by an offering of water poured out on the temple rock, the miracle of the exodus,

the water springing out of the rock.

The rock which, according to rabbinical tradition, followed Israel in the desert.

"If anyone thirst,
let him come to me;
and let him drink,

who believes in me!"
"As the Scripture says:
'Out of his heart will flow rivers of living water.' "
This rock where Israel quenched their third, Lord,
was it you? (Ex. 17:1–7; Ps. 105:41; I Cor. 10:4.)
And the sanctuary, the altar whence the prophet
sees springing forth
the River of life,
is it your body which you gave? (Ezek. 47:1–12; John
19:34–35; I John 5:6–7.)
Springing forth of the Spirit into the heart of your
church for the quickening of the world.

"WHO IS THIS MAN?"

Prophet? Messiah? Who is this man? Where was he
born?
The discussion takes up again; it will go on till the
end of time.
Until he appears in the glory of his Reign.
Then "every eye shall see him."

No one dares lay a hand on him—in broad daylight.
The crowd is too excited.
The hour decided of God has not yet struck.

"No man ever spoke like this man!"
Jesus' very best witnesses are now the police.
Irony of the Pharisees: "Have you let yourselves be
taken in, also?"
What does this Jerusalem "scum" know about spir-
itual things?

Nicodemus, honest judge that he is, demands that the law be heeded; that this man be heard and judged according to the facts. But what can an honest man do in the face of unchained passions?

His colleagues make fun: **"Are you from Galilee too? Try studying a little! You'll see that no prophet comes from Galilee!"**

The partisan spirit knows no other kind of argument.

Arguments which prove nothing but which hang a heavy threat over the defender's head.

It seems that after this Nicodemus said no more.

What can a just man do against passion?

He can do something only if he is ready to go to the bitter end, ready to get himself involved,

ready to die for his convictions.

The case is put off till later.
Each goes to his own home.

THE WOMAN TAKEN IN ADULTERY
John 8:1–11

The Temple court. The circle of accusers. The woman in the midst. Jesus silently writing in the sand with his finger.

They are waiting. The silence weighs heavy.

"Let him who is without sin among you cast the first stone."

Jesus goes back to his writing. His silence is heavier than words.

They have become silent, also. They have left, **"one by one, beginning with the eldest."**

Becoming older means knowing oneself better. Logic would dictate that the older we become the less we judge.

Only one is without sin. Only one would have the right to judge. And he abstains.

Because he came not to judge men, but to save them.

"Neither do I condemn you; go, and do not sin again."

A future opens to this woman who had no more future.

A new beginning made possible:
for this woman;
for these men suddenly reduced to silence;
for you, whoever you may be, whom the strength of
temptation has made to stumble,
for all of us, poor pharisaical Christianity.

Lord, if we contemplated this scene more often,
if we knew how to listen to your silence,
how many attitudes would be changed?

"I AM"

John 8:12–59

The controversy takes up again between Jesus and the Pharisees. Their opposition is becoming more and more immovable.

The declarations Jesus is making are of a nature to take away all ambiguity: He is the Light of the World. He alone knows the Father. He alone is enabled to deliver men from the slavery of sin. Three times he claims as his own the sacred name used strictly for God only: "I AM" [2c] (Ex. 3:14).

And now the discussion takes a new turn: Jesus disputes his adversaries' right to the title they count as their highest glory: their position as children of Abraham. By rejecting the promised Heir, they show themselves to be "children of the devil," of him who is by nature a liar and a murderer.

The breach is complete. The die has been cast. Already the final clash seems inevitable.

And thus, one step after another, John unfolds before our eyes what to him is nothing less than God on trial.

"I am the Light of the World;
he who follows me will not walk in darkness,
but will have the light of life."
"He who follows me . . ." All is here. To follow
Jesus is to have "the light of life." Light does not have
to give any proof for itself; it shines, it enlightens, it is
there.

Light and darkness: ancient symbols of life and death.

In the Day of God, his light will enlighten and trans-
figure the world.
Flame of truth which will consume all our lies.
Flame of justice which will consume all our iniquity.
Flame of love which will consume all our hate.
There will be no more night.

This Day has long been expected, announced by the
prophets:
"Arise, shine; for your light has come,
and the glory of the Lord has risen upon you,
while darkness covers the earth,
and thick darkness the peoples.
But the Lord will arise upon you,
and his glory will be seen upon you.
Nations shall come to your light,
and kings to the brightness of your coming." (Isa.
60:1–3.)
Jesus declares that he is fulfilling this immense expectation.

No one who has been nourished from the Scriptures could mistake the meaning of his words.

THE TESTIMONY DISPUTED

The Pharisees have not mistaken his meaning, either.

What they are disputing is his all-encompassing claim, the validity of his testimony:

"You are bearing witness to yourself; your testimony is not valid." [5] (Cf. Deut. 17:6.)

The inquiry will go on from age to age.

Unbelief asks for proof. But it receives none other than Jesus himself: his sovereign authority, his sovereign liberty, and the works that his Father does by him.

To listen to him, believe him, follow him, means passing from darkness to light: that cannot be proved, it must be lived.

Mysterious assurance of him who alone knows whence he has come, and where he is going.

And now the insidious question is asked again:

"Where is your father?"

—**"You know neither me nor my Father."**

A terrible judgment: these guardians of the faith *do not know God.*

They do not *recognize* him in the One he has sent.

These words Jesus spoke in the Temple. **"But no one arrested him, because his hour had not yet come."**

No one is master of that hour but God.

Nevertheless time is short and his departure is at hand:
**"I go away, and you will seek me
and you will die in your sin.
Where I am going,
you cannot come."**
There is only one place where his adversaries im-
agine they could not find him, in the hades of suicide!
Again and always those two worlds with no common
meeting place: the world of **"up there"** and the world
of **"down here."**

**"When you have lifted up the Son of Man,
then you will know that I AM,
and that I do nothing on my own authority,
but what my Father has taught me,
that I say."**
These men who are accusing him will cause him to
be lifted up—on the cross and in glory. Then his
identity will be manifest.
He is He who is, the Lord.
The sacred name of Sinai takes the form of a man.

Unutterable mystery of the gracious condescension of
God.—Or blasphemy and scandal. There is no neutral
ground.

Just now we are told that **"many believed in him."**
Will Jesus sustain this beginning of faith?
No, he will unmask its fragility.

ABRAHAM AND JESUS CHRIST

**"If you continue in my word,
you are truly my disciples,
you will know the truth**

71

and the truth will make you free."

"Continue" implies perseverance, ceaselessness.

One must listen **"as those who are disciples"** (Isa. 50:4), in order to obey.

He who thus walks in the faith, **"will know."** [8]

Knowing, in the Bible vocabulary, implies a total involvement of the entire being. A mutual penetration.

This *truth,* that is to be known, is nothing abstract, no wisdom, no gnosis limited to a few initiates. It is Someone.

It has a name: Jesus Christ.

For he is **"the Way, the Truth and the Life."**

Jesus Christ—truth lived out.

He in whom the reality of man, the reality of God, the reality of the world, are revealed to us.[10]

The only one who has ever been truly free. The only one capable of freeing.

We must not fail to notice this progression from the word heard and received to obedience, from obedience to knowledge, from knowledge to freedom. For such is the pulse of Christian life.

His listeners lash out at him: **"We are descendants of Abraham, and have never been in bondage to anyone!"**

Again the controversy breaks out between the sons of Abraham according to the flesh and the sons of Abraham according to the spirit.

Tradition cannot take the place of faith. Our ancestors' faith cannot save us.

But even more serious: they will accuse us in the Last Day.

Abraham's children are blind and deaf; the Heir according to the promise is before them, and they only think of putting him to death.

For there is nothing that he wants more than to tear them away from their security.

"Slaves of sin": sin seen as something that holds our entire being; that takes over our lives with a complete mastery; that secretly, subtly, commands them.

We consider ourselves members of the Household; and Another is already in possession of us.

Only One is "Son in his own home."
"So if the Son makes you free,
you will be free indeed."

Unique freedom of the one on whom the "prince of this world" has no hold.

Royal liberty of the Son,

come to invite all men to the feast of life:

the tax gatherers, and the prostitutes, and the Samaritans,

but also the Pharisees.

All are invited; and the door he opens, no one can shut;

but one can refuse to enter in.

The opponents, here, are the spurious believers of all time;

"born" of the race of Abraham or "born" within Christianity,

but who have never been penetrated by the word of life.

Slaves who deny their slavery and who, for this reason, can never be free.

They claim as theirs the ancestor they have denied, they have not believed the promises of God and *today* his grace is hidden from them.

Here the Lord is bringing an exceptionally serious accusation.

It is no longer a question of ignorance or of ill will, but of deliberate refusal. A conscious rejection of truth.

Two kingdoms clash: *God's* and *Satan's*.

He who is by nature life and truth,
he who is by nature murder and lies.

And each one's works carry his own signature.

Jesus accused of being "a Samaritan" or "demon-possessed."

Heresy or madness: the supreme arguments ever used to eliminate bothersome prophets.

**"Truly, truly, I say to you,
if anyone keeps my word,
he will never see death."**

Irony is the Jews' stock-in-trade: **"Are you greater than Abraham, our father?"**

The same question forever coming back: *Who are you?* It comes back again and again throughout the gospel with intentional emphasis. For in this question is concentrated the entire controversy between Jews and Christians.

In fact it is THE QUESTION, the only one that has ever counted.

Then and now.

"Your Father Abraham rejoiced

74

at the thought of seeing My Day
he saw it and was glad."
Abraham, long in advance the father of all the freed.
For he believed God's promises. By faith he contemplated the Day of God.
And this Day has come.

"Before Abraham was, I AM."
The mystery of this word: the eternal Son, present in the world from the beginning of time.
The Son of Man, human face of the holy God;
before whose image we were thought, desired, created.

Naïve anthropomorphism, profound intuition?
God takes on human form to visit the world;
makes the man and the woman with his own hands;
calls them in the garden;
takes the form of angels to visit Abraham, his friend;
wrestles with Jacob and dislocates his hip:
"I have seen God face to face and have been preserved" (Gen. 32:24–30);
speaks face to face with Moses, **"as a man speaks to his friend"** (Ex. 33:11).

The flaming chariot of Ezekiel: above the four animals a firmament, above the firmament a throne; and on the throne, **"a being as it were of human form"** (Ezek. 1:26).
Daniel's vision: **"One like a Son of Man coming on the clouds of heaven."**
"To him was given dominion
and glory and kingdom,
and all peoples, nations, and languages served him."
(Dan. 7:13–14.)

We must not lift too high the veil of these appearances,
  discreet foreshadowing of the incarnation.
  The mystery must be believed—mystery of the Son
in the bosom of the Father,
  from the beginning of time,
  the same yesterday, today, and forever.

**"Before Abraham was,
I am."**
Then they took up stones to throw at him.
The split is complete.
Such an assertion is such that Jesus must either be
believed or be stoned.

LIGHT AND DARKNESS
John, Ch. 9

The healing of the man blind from birth, a sign granted to faith. But a sign of utter ruin for those who do not believe.

The one who has come to the light.[7] Opposite, those who say they see and are blind:

physical blindness, symbol of another blindness, more deadly.

THE HEALING OF THE MAN BLIND FROM BIRTH

"As he passed by, he saw a man blind from his birth."
A man blind from birth: a man whose darkness has never been pierced by any light. He has no acquaintance with the beauty of the world: the brightness of spring, the glory of autumn; a human face luminous with tenderness.

The disciples see the problem: "Who has sinned?" All they can think of is establishing the guilty parties.

Jesus, on the other hand, sees the man. And in this man not his past, but his future,

the glory of God is about to be manifested.
For Jesus has not come to talk about evil, but to abolish it.

"In that day the deaf shall hear the words of the book,
and out of their gloom and darkness
the eyes of the blind shall see." (Isa. 29:18.)

"I AM, and I have called you in righteousness,
I have taken you by the hand and formed you,
I have given you as a covenant to the people and as a light to the nations,
to open the eyes of the blind,
to bring out the prisoners from the dungeon,
from the prison those who sit in darkness." (Isa. 42:6–7.)
The dawn of the Messianic era clearly prefigured.

"As long as it is day . . ."
Jesus emphasizes that his time is short.
"Night comes when no one can work."
Night of Calvary and of betrayal.
Night of death.
Night of a world closed up to God's love.
Night when it seems that the adversary is victorious.
And you, O church, work also, "while it is day."
For you, also, time is short.
Doors that were open yesterday are today closed.
Occasions thrown away are never regained.
Perhaps your days, also, are numbered?

"As long as I am in the world,
I am the Light of the World."

Strange words, Lord: are they no longer true?
—Yes, they are, but only the look of faith perceives it.
The flame has passed into your hands.
Through you my glory must shine forth,
my love must become flesh.
Henceforth, my church, it is your task to restore sight
to the blind, speech to the dumb.

The healing of the blind man astonishes his neighbors.
Questions are asked, discussions had, comments made.
The man is led to the competent authorities.
And the Pharisees launch the inquiry—
prudently.
But the verdict has already been decided beforehand.

The parents evade all questions.
There is no reason for being on bad terms with the
synagogue.

The man himself sticks to the facts.
What he knows is that now he *can see.*
We know God by his acts, by the gracious gifts we
receive from him.
Only what has been lived rings true.

The Pharisees insist. And this time the man unmasks
their insincerity.
His answer is not without irony: "What! You who
know everything, you do not know where this man is
from who has opened my eyes?"
He answers them with their own arguments: **"If this
man were not from God, he could do nothing."**
There is no limit to the anger of these doctors of the
law:

"You were born in utter sin, and you are trying to teach us something!"
And they cast him out.

And now a second miracle is performed.
Once again, in the path of the blind man, out of the fugitive's guise,
    the Son of Man stands forth.
What was the sun's light compared with this other light, now bathing him in its joy?
    " 'Lord, I believe,' and he worshiped him."

THE JUDGMENT

"For judgment I came into this world:
that those who do not see may see,
and that those who see may become blind."

Limitless mercy for those born blind; for those who have never seen the light from God shining on their pathway:
    the ignorant; the honest unbelievers of all time;
    all those who do not know they are loved of God.

A heavy sentence for those who "know"—who pretend they know:
    men acquainted with all the subtleties of theology and casuistry,
    —but who have no love.
Men fearfully sure of their salvation, who are not astonished at the freeness of grace.
    "If you were blind,
    you would be without sin;

80

but you say, 'We see!'
and your sin remains."
Fearful warning to the religious of all time.
For, by a strange reversal of things, it may be that
those who call themselves believers are the blind, and
the blind just may become the ones with eyes to see?
"He came to his own home,
and his own received him not.
But to all who received him,
he gave power to become children of God."

We see Jesus looking for those he is going to make his,
at the crossing of all the world's roads.
Lambs abandoned by false shepherds,
which only his love has been able to find.

The Samaritan woman, the paralytic, the man blind
from birth,
living symbols of God's willing grace—
living symbols which are to become, in the faith of
the catacombs, the triple symbol
of new birth, of the mystery of baptism.

THE PASTOR OF THE FLOCK
John, Ch. 10

THE SHEPHERD'S MISSION

The ancient symbol of the shepherd, never changing since the time of Abel.

Shepherds of the Mesopotamian plains: Abraham and his flocks.

Shepherds of the Judean desert: David seizing the lion's prey from its very mouth.

Shepherds of Bethlehem.

Shepherds moving flocks to the Alps, to the Pyrenees.

A flock to feed—no small task.

You have to know the terrain, where the good grass is found, the watering places.

You have to seek out the lost, care for the wounded, carry the lambs.

Confidence must reign between the shepherd and the flock.

The true shepherd knows his sheep and they follow him.

He calls them by name.

GOD, SHEPHERD OF ISRAEL

Cleaving the Red Sea for them to pass,
marching before them through the desert;
feeding them with manna and water from the rock
("and this rock was Christ"),
opening up for his people the Promised Land.

The pilgrim has gone up to the Holy City.
He has offered the stiplated lambs.
The table is set before him. He partakes of the meal.
He takes of the oil of joy, the wine of life.
He heads back to his lot: loneliness and danger,
his soul rested, his heart joyful:
"THE LORD IS MY SHEPHERD."

Soon another sacrifice will be offered.
Another Table will be set
and the blood will flow from the Shepherd's side.

**" 'Woe to the shepherds who destroy and scatter the
sheep of my pasture!' says the Lord.**
**" 'You have scattered my flock, you have driven them
away,**
and you have not attended to them:
Behold, I will attend to you for your evildoings.' "

. . . .

**"Woe to the shepherds of Israel who have been
feeding themselves." . . . "The weak you have not
strengthened, the sick you have not healed, the crippled
you have not bound up, the strayed you have not
brought back, the lost you have not sought, and with
force and harshness you have ruled them." . . . "Be-**

hold, I myself will search for my sheep." . . . "I will make my sheep to lie down . . . ; I will gather them together. . . . I will seek the lost, and I will bring back the strayed, and I will bind up the crippled, and I will heal the sick." . . . "And I will set up over them one shepherd, my servant David, and he shall feed them: he shall feed them and be their shepherd." . . . "My servant David shall be prince among them . . .

"I will make with them a covenant of peace . . ." (Jer. 23:1–6; Ezek. 34:2,4,11,13,16,23–25).

Kings of long ago, leaders of today—all included in one judgment.

You have drunk the milk of the flock, enriched yourselves at its expense, you have done everything but watch over it.

And now the flock is taken from you.

You have let my sheep wander away. Even worse: you *chased* them away.

You have let thieves make of them their prey. And when wild beasts attacked them, you fled.

I am, Pharisees deaf and blind, the new David often predicted.

King not yet crowned,
who must defend his threatened flock
with only the sling of faith—and his life to give.

"I am," says Jesus, "the door of the sheep,
if anyone enters by me, he will be saved,
and will go in and out and will find pasture."
Jesus, the only means of entering the Father's house.

He who enters through him is "saved": saved from judgment; out of the enemy's reach.

84

He is not locked up in the fold; he is on the contrary free—free with a marvelous freedom.

He comes and goes at will. As a child of the household. (Cf. John 8:35–36.)

The true shepherd **"lays down his life for his sheep."**
Here Jesus announces plainly his death and the meaning of this death.

For it is through his death that he will make us participants in his life.

In his fullness. In his freedom.

**"I know my sheep
and my sheep know me,
as the Father knows me
and I know the Father."** [8]
The knowledge that the Father has of the Son, that the Son has of the Father:

perfect communion of will and of love.

Being known of Jesus Christ: seen, read, accepted, called, wanted, loved.

Knowing him: recognizing his voice, loving him, following him.

Intimacy which slowly penetrates to the very depths of the being.

**"For this reason the Father loves me,
because I lay down my life,
that I may take it again.
No one takes it from me,
but I lay it down of my own accord.
I have power to lay it down,
and I have power to take it again;
this charge I have received from my Father."**

The Father wanted the Son to be given. But he gave himself freely.
For the offering of love can only be a life freely given.
But he who gives it here has "the power to take it again."
Death endured, conquered, surmounted,
once and for all.
Its sting taken away.

"I have other sheep,
that are not of this fold;
I must bring them also,
and they will heed my voice;
there will be one flock,
one shepherd."
The great gathering-in has begun,
and only eternity will see it ended.

Lord, how many are there in the plains of Asia, in the tropics of Africa,
    in our cities,
    who have never heard the Shepherd's voice?
    We have jealously cared for our respective folds;
    our select flocks.
    We have set up our doors and our ticket offices.
    Lord, when will we learn that there is only one door and only one doorkeeper?
    When will we be one flock under one shepherd?

Lord, I think of all who have been wounded by life
whom you have placed in my path,
and whom I have served poorly,
whom I have loved insufficiently.
Oh, Lord! When will you give our hearts
the dimensions of yours?

THE FEAST OF THE DEDICATION

The Feast of the Dedication: memorial of the purification of the Temple by Judas Maccabaeus.

But it is not the external desecrations that count.

Another has come. And now the Temple itself is to be challenged.

And it is around this Other Man that everything is revolving today.

"How long will you keep us in suspense? If you are the Christ, tell us plainly."

The Jews recognized the reference to the new David, to the Shepherd of Israel, who can be no other than the Messiah.

The big question has now been asked.

"I myself will judge between sheep and sheep, between rams and goats" . . . **"between the fat sheep and the lean sheep."** (Ezek. 34:17,20.)

The dividing line forms itself naturally and alone. Jesus can add nothing to the signs already given. The true sheep, the ones given to him by the Father, recognize his voice and follow him.

And *nothing* else can tear them from his hand.

For being in the Son's hand is equivalent to being in the Father's hand.

**"I and the Father
are one."**
The Jews took up stones to stone him.

. . . .

"You, being only a man, make yourself God."

87

From a Jew's point of view, there is no worse blasphemy. And the condemnation is legitimate.

Jesus refers his position to the only authority recognized by the Jews: Holy Scripture. Is it not written there concerning the magistrates—those who have heard the Word of God, **"You are gods, you are all sons of the Most High"**? (Ps. 58:1; 82:6.)

The argument is rabbinical and subtle: if those who have heard the Word are called gods, how much more so the Messenger who is the Word, and whose works carry the signature of the Sender.

And thus, during this feast of the consecration of the Temple, also called the Feast of Lights, the Son declares himself to be the *true Consecrated One,* he in whom Israel's destiny finds its fulfillment.[2e]

The Light shines but men want nothing to do with it.

Jesus leaves Judea, goes "across the Jordan," and there, we are told, **"many believed in him."** The Gospel writer feels the necessity of emphasizing that those who now believe have once received John's baptism and thus his testimony is confirmed: **"Everything he said about this man was true."**

THE LAST SIGN:
THE RESURRECTION OF LAZARUS
John 11:1–54

In the progression of the Fourth Gospel the resurrection of Lazarus is the last of the signs used by Jesus to manifest his glory during his earthly ministry. It is also the one that will hasten his condemnation.

> **"The hour is coming**
> **when all who are in the tomb**
> **will hear his voice and come forth."** (John 5:28.)

Jesus is master of the elements, master over sickness. But he is also master over death.

The death and the resurrection of Lazarus thus become announcement, and as it were, prefiguration of the death and resurrection of the Lord himself; and of all the "living" in the Last Day.

BETHANY

"Jesus loved Martha and her sister and Lazarus."
Mary and Martha are assumed to be known to the reader. (Luke 10:38–42; John 12:1–8.) We know nothing of Lazarus except that he was their brother, and that Jesus **"loved him,"** also.

89

Jesus was acquainted with the sweetness of a friendly home where he was taken in, loved, understood almost without speaking.

The vocation of the Son of God does not exclude human affection in its authentic manifestations, so special, so simple.

Jesus has *friends*.

"Lord, he whom you love is ill."

The heart's cry toward the one who *can* heal.

But Jesus does not come. Purposely he waits two days where he is. He lets death do its work.

And all in order that the Father's glory may shine brighter . . .

Lord, my faith and my love run afoul of such words. How obscure your ways are occasionally.

The apparent silence of God before suffering and death. Before the absurdity of certain deaths . . .

Will all that be explained, someday?

Freedom of the Son, who knows his hour, and when the day is bright and when the night comes, is always in charge.

"If you had been here. . . ."

Jesus' answer is ambiguous—as is so often the case in this Gospel; future resurrection, immediate resurrection? **"Your brother will rise again."**

And this ambiguousness, deeply felt by Martha, leads to a new revelation:

"I AM the resurrection and the life."

"He who believes in me, though he die, yet shall he live;

90

**and whoever lives and believes in me,
shall never die.
Do you believe this?"**

What has been hinted at throughout the Gospel is now explicitly revealed: eternal life is not an "over there" beyond physical death, it is, for the one who believes, present participation in the life of him who lives forever.

Communion that nothing can destroy.

Martha answers with a confession of faith:

"Yes, Lord, I believe that you are the Christ, the Son of God, he who is coming into the world."

We are not immortal souls as ancient wisdom would have it.

We have been rescued from death by the grace of Christ alone.

So the certainty of my resurrection rests wholly on the fact that he is the resurrection and the life.

Belief in the Son of God means believing in the resurrection of the world.

Far beyond all death and all despair.

Lord, grant us to believe you. For we can obtain this impossible faith only if it is given to us.

Our twentieth century strongly resembles the Greek world which, at the mention of the word "resurrection," politely went its way, if it did not stop to make fun: **"We will hear you about this some other time"** (Acts 17:32).

John is acquainted with this resistance.

91

And it is very precisely here—concerning this problem of the resurrection—that the cleavage is to appear between faith and unbelief.

Jesus, seeing Mary cry, **"was deeply moved in his spirit."**
The Greek word implies, even more than pain, indignation and anger.
This is the only time, Lord, that we see you weeping and trembling at the sight of death.
Is not death, every time it occurs, a victory of the enemy over the God of life?
of that enemy whom you are going to meet in personal combat, and conquer at the price of great personal agony?
of that enemy who has made men weep since the begining of time
and will make them weep until the end? Is it not written:
"The last enemy to be conquered is death" (I Cor. 15: 26; Rev. 21:3–4)?

Until the end death's cold will chill men's hearts,
until the end they will know the rending of separation.
Lord, that is still true, even if we believe in the resurrection;
and how much more so if we do not believe.
Did you not take the measure of all this with one glance? of the immense challenge thrown out by the prince of death to the Prince of life?

"If you believe, you will see the glory[11] of God!"
The glory of God made manifest at the very heart of death. Here resides the paradox of Christianity.

Glory of Easter. The dead unbound from their wrappings.

Unbound by the crucified God who takes upon himself their death.

All this is only predicted in Lazarus.

ONE MUST DIE FOR ALL THE NATION!

One must die for all the nation!
The Pharisees and the Sadducees, brothers and enemies, form a coalition in view of the common danger: **"This man performs many signs. If we let him go on in this way, everyone will believe in him and the Romans will come and destroy both our place and our nation."**
The question of truth has faded into the background. It is not even considered anymore. Political considerations come before everything else. The existence of Judaism, the liberty of the country, are threatened.

Strange powerlessness of the establishment facing a bothersome prophet who, for his part, acts . . .

And now Caiaphas breaks in: **"You know nothing at all; you do not understand that it is expedient for you that one man should die for the nation, and that the whole nation should not perish."**
It is in the interest of the chosen people, it is in the interest of the entire nation that this man perish!

Caiaphas is telling the truth, the Gospel writer adds. Because of his office, unawares, he is, in speaking these words, the mouth of God.

Tomorrow the establishment will be swept away.

93

But faithful or not, it will to the end serve God's purpose.

Such is God's strange way of doing things.

But God's purpose goes farther than Caiaphas thinks: Jesus has not come only to save his own people.

He has other sheep in other pastures: the great gathering-in of the promise is about to begin.

Jesus, aware that his days are numbered, withdraws one last time to be alone with his disciples.

THE HOUR HAS COME
John 11:55 to 12:50

"The Passover of the Jews was at hand."
This is the third Passover mentioned in John.
At the first the Temple was purified and the new temple was announced.
The second is tied in with the miracle of the loaves and fish and with Jesus' proclamation as the bread of life.
This time the hour of fulfillment has struck.

The multitude of pilgrims are going up to the Holy City to immerse themselves in the rites of purification. One question is on every tongue: "Will Jesus come up to the feast or not?"
It is known that his arrest has been officially ordered.

SIX DAYS BEFORE THE PASSOVER

God bless you, Mary, for feeling with sure intuition that his hour has come,
God bless you for this loving act, for this purest nard, for this ointment poured forth on him who is to die;
God bless you for this senseless waste,

senseless in men's eyes; in God's eyes precious.

Lord, grant us a bit of folly for our narrow hearts, which, so often, count the cost.

You did no such counting.

THE TRIUMPHAL ENTRY

Procession, palm branches, and singing.
The King enters into his city.

Jesus fulfills the ancient prophecy:
"Rejoice greatly, O daughter of Zion!
Shout aloud, O daughter of Jerusalem!
Lo, your king comes to you:
righteous and victorious is he,
humble and riding on an ass,
on a colt the foal of an ass." (Zech. 9:9.)
The multitude begins singing the Hallel and acclaims the king:

> Oh, Lord, stoop down and save us!
> Oh, Lord, give us success!

Yes, your Savior is coming. But not for the success you are counting on.

His royal crown will be made of thorns.

The branches: reminder of the crownings of yesteryear. Announcement of the Kingdom to come.

Strange provocation, which will hasten events on to their fatal end.

Prefiguration of the day when the King of Glory
will enter into a redeemed Zion,

96

of the day when all creatures will sing as with one voice
the hosanna of faith.

AND HE IS LIFTED UP

You impatient Greeks who want to see Jesus, leave him
with his own for a few more hours.

The incarnate Son is a man of one country and of one
people: **"Salvation comes from the Jews."** He has eaten
from Israel's life-giving vine, and he owes Israel the last
days of his life.

He owes them to his apostles, to those who believe in
him. To those who will perhaps yet believe.

Everything must happen at the very heart of the
chosen people: the last discussions; the final betrayal,
and the condemnation.

"The hour has come
for the Son of Man
to be glorified."
This hour has been prepared by the entire gospel.[6]
It has not yet come . . .
It is coming . . .
AND now it is upon us.
This hour that cuts the world's history in two
(and the world will let it pass unawares),
The hour when the beloved Son is to be lifted up,
on the infamous cross, between two robbers.
The hour of glorification.
The grain must "die" to bring forth fruit.
Jesus makes this requirement into the law of life.
The grain that does not die stays *alone.*

Solitude of the ego. Solitude of a life concentrated in
itself.

Tragedy of the lost paradise where man, thinking he was finding himself, lost others and himself as well.

Existence doomed to sterility. For the worm is at the heart of all the fruit it bears;

thus, it ends up only in a vacuum.

(*The Fall,* by Camus.)

Jesus Christ: the mystery of a life totally open and given.

Given to God. Given to men.

He invites us to the grace, to the fullness of such a life.

Joy of a given life.

We feel that such a life can exist, Lord. But to follow you, we must be ready to drop everything.

And how many times we have backed off.

"Where I am, there shall my servant be." The path of abasement which alone leads to glory. That, Lord, is exactly what we are afraid of.

"If anyone serves me, my Father will honor him."

Those whom the Father **"will honor"** are not always those whom we would choose. Humble lives, hidden men and women, lives given drop by drop, not even aware of their greatness. Whom the world has not known.

Fruits of love, known only of God.

"Now my soul is troubled.

And what shall I say?

'Father, save me from this hour?'

No, I have come purposely for this hour.

Father, glorify your name!"

98

The only reminder in The Gospel According to John of the combat in Gethsemane.

The Father's will long since known, accepted.

Extreme discretion concerning the combat waged. But it underlies the entire Gospel.

Jesus knows the fright of abandonment, of betrayal, of death.

He knows them because he is a man and suffers them in his flesh.

He knows them for another reason because he is the Son of God and can alone measure the depth of our hells.

Jesus alone knows whence he has come, where he is going.

Paschal lamb, predestined from the beginning for this offering, for *THIS HOUR,* when he will take upon himself the world's sin.

"Then a voice came from heaven."

The Father's seal on the work of his Son. The Father glorifying himself—*revealing* himself in this supreme humiliation.

Glory and the cross. Two faces of the same truth.[11]

All-powerfulness of crucified love.

The hour has come when the world is to be judged. Unmasked.

When the **"prince of this world"** will throw in his last terrible card,

deploy all his forces in the assault of the beloved Son.

They will all be there, beating the wooden gibbet with their staccato rhythm;

hate, denouncement, unconcern, and cowardice.

Hate which, through the Son, reaches God.
Our humanity forever laid bare.
When truth, justice, holiness, love, took on flesh,
we crucified them.
Judgment of the world: the world's judgment of itself.
Voluntary deicide, calculated, carried out. Failed.

Failed.
The prince of this world **"cast down."**
The accuser thrown out from before God.
Life stronger than death, love triumphing over hate.
The Son standing erect,
answering for man before the Father's throne.

Man—I am he. I conquered the world. I conquered
it once and for all on this cross set up by your blind
madness.

Nailed to this cross I am calling you, I am waiting
for you.

Here are my flesh and my blood, given for you.

Believe this pardon. Be born into this love.

It is a crucified God who is holding his arms out to
you.

**"When I am lifted up from the earth, I will draw all
men to myself."**
ALL MEN.

Brother, whoever you are, this promise, this call, are
for you.

Tremendous statement.

They will come from everywhere, from the east and
from the west, from the north and from the south. The
prophet's vision fulfilled, surpassed.

Light from the cross which will pierce through all
the world's opaqueness.

"**All men!**" Lord, can we hope that someday all resistance will be broken? Will your cross, like a mighty magnet, draw to you all the skeptics, all the rebellious, all the hopeless of the world, and even those who crucified you?

"**Every eye will see him, even those who pierced him.**" (Rev. 1:7.) Great and terrible day when all will know who you are;

when all will contemplate the glory of crucified divinity;

when, conscious of the miserable state of their love, believers and unbelievers will weep at your feet.

WHO HAS BELIEVED OUR WORDS?

Jesus announces his death, salvation for the world. But the crowd neither understands nor believes. It escapes in sterile arguments, repeated a hundred times: if you were the Messiah, you could not die. Your words are obscure . . .

Jesus cuts them off. There is not much time left. The decision must be made today.

It will soon be night. Night of death. Night of unbelief:

"**He who walks in darkness does not know where he is going.**"

Characteristic of the world in which we live: apparently so sure of itself, so uncertain of tomorrow. A world not knowing where it is going, neither in whom or in what it believes.

Light from Jesus Christ.

Take hold of it while it shines. Refuse not God's *today.*

Be a son of the light in a world surrounded by darkness on all sides.

Light of saving love.

"Who has believed our words?"

John, faced with the mystery of the Jews' unbelief— and this mystery continues still when he is writing— sends them to their own Scriptures, to the prophet Isaiah.

The figure of the Servant of Isaiah, ch. 53: who, while he was living, believed in his message and in the efficacy of his sacrifice? Who recognizes him today in this Son whom he prophetically proclaimed?

And did not God himself predict this future blindness of the chosen people to his prophet at the same time when He revealed to him his glory and consecrated him for his mission? (Isa., ch. 6.)

Thus, all is foreseen, desired, directed by the Almighty who holds history in his hand.

My God, God of Jesus Christ, is it possible that you yourself, sometimes blind our eyes and harden our hearts? Must we *touch bottom* before your grace goes into action?

Or must we simply understand that your word hardens, closes up the one who consciously rejects it?

Darkness of crucifixion day when final and complete rejection takes place and becomes the means of a peace even more complete.

Lord, we are too small to understand these things.

102

There are some who do not believe. There are some who believe and who do not say so. Theirs is the greatest guilt.

They do not speak out, John tells us, **"for fear of being cast out of the synagogue."** Institution more sacred than truth. Institution, but also the prestige attached to it in men's eyes; a complete set of social rules.

John's judgment is brief and brutal: **"They loved the praise of men more than the praise of God."**

Jesus speaks again. And once again it is to witness to his Father.

His total dependence confirmed once again.

Men are judged, not by him, but by the refusal they throw up against light, by this Word come from God, which is grace and life.

Judgment is meted out on him who, having *heard* the word, did not guard it.

Nothing is said of the others.

Meeting Jesus Christ is every man's **"hour"**; the only one that counts, in time and for eternity.

THE SERVANT
John, Ch. 13

"Knowing that his hour had come . . ." [12]
Jesus "knows." He knows when the hour has come.
The hour of separation. The hour of returning to his
Father.

He knows Judas is to betray him.
He knows Peter is to deny him.
And yet **"he loved them to the end."**

THE LAST MEAL

Taking off his outer garments, girding himself with
a towel: such is the classic garb of a servant. The Hebrew
servant was not asked to wash his master's feet: this
service was considered too humiliating.

The wife washed her husband's feet.

The King of Israel, the Lord of the earth, the Husband of the Church kneels before his own and washes
their feet.

Symbolic act of him who came not to domineer but
to serve;

of him who came to die the ignominious death of a
slave to wash away the world's iniquity.

104

Peter sees only the act, not its meaning. And refuses to let himself be served in that way. And then, a moment later, wants much more.

Unseasonable zeal which causes us to always want something else or something more than the proffered grace.

Believe the grace of your baptism. Live it. That is enough.

The way of voluntary humiliation opened up by the Lord so that his disciples may make it theirs:

"If I, your Lord and Master, have washed your feet, you also ought to wash one another's feet."

The Son's glory is in taking on the form of a servant; man's glory is to obtain titles and honors.

Jesus has seen the thirst for prestige ruin the religious leaders of his time. He knows the temptations awaiting his church. He puts his closest friends on their guard.

Christian service implies humility just as much as love; the humility of true love.

That is why our so-called "welfare" works are too often only a travesty of the service Jesus had in mind. For they honor the giver and humiliate the receiver.

Our day no longer puts up with almsgiving—of any kind. It wants justice, and rightly so. But we no longer know what love is: the love that does not count how much it costs to give;

the love that washes respectfully the dusty feet of the wayfarer.

The slave used to accept subordination to his master as part of the way things were.

The Christian accepts subordination to everyone. Because it is a part of the way things are *for him*.

105

The sin of men, of nations, of races, who think themselves superior has been to mistake domination for service. Their "service" has thus been false from the roots up. And they wonder why they fail.

Mutual submissiveness is so contrary to human nature that in order to accept it, all of Christ's grace, and his example, must intervene.

"I have given you an example, that you also should do as I have done to you." "If you know these things, blessed are you if you do them."

JUDAS

Betrayal at the very heart of the cenacle. The greatest mystery of the entire Gospel. A mystery that we will never penetrate.

**"Even my bosom friend
in whom I trusted and who ate of my bread
has lifted his heel against me."** (Ps. 41:9.)

Did the Son of God have to know that he was to be abandoned so many times, even this last time?

Do we have to know that the house of God is never completely sheltered from the demon's attacks?

Jesus, **"troubled in spirit."** Jesus, knowing that betrayal is imminent, does nothing to stop it. He even hastens it on.

Judas takes with him the bread dipped in wine: last sign of grace or of condemnation?

And he is swallowed up by the night.

God is accomplishing his work, and Satan his. But Satan, throughout, in spite of himself, is God's instrument. Working for our salvation.

106

THE DEPARTURE DRAWS NEAR

Judas' exit announces the imminence of the passion. But John gives us to understand that in a very deep sense everything is already accomplished. The death, the betrayal, are already accepted. The anguish has been surmounted. The victory is won. The Son has glorified the Father, the Father has glorified the Son in his humiliation, he will soon glorify him by granting him eternal glory.

The particularity of Christ according to John: the battle is situated *before* the final ending. We can already see the crucified Christ haloed with his coming glory. He will never depart from his sovereign liberty.

The church's life originates in this victory. The martyrs' agony is illuminated by this victory.

We are at the limit of eternity and time.

But the disciples are still in time. They are going to sink deep into the anguish and uncertainty of separation. The Lord knows this. With infinite tenderness and tactfulness he prepares them for the inevitable deprivation which will soon leave them orphans.

He gives them a **"new commandment."** Leaving them, he gives them to each other. He gives them a love that is to reflect his.
"Yes, even as I have loved you,
you also, love one another."
Love that asks nothing, love that endures all; love ready to give its life.

Love that accepts the other man and believes in his future. His future being prepared for him by God's grace.

Love that sees in every other person one of God's hopes.

Communion of brothers in the Son. Marvelous companionship divine.

"By this all men will know that you are my disciples."
Touchstone of any community calling itself Christian.

Simon—determined to follow his Lord anywhere, ready to give up his life.

And he probably would have given it up if it had been a question of going down fighting.

Simon—full of illusions as to his own strength. No warning does any good. Only the downfall will, at last, teach him to know himself.

The Lord, knowing this, will be waiting for him at that bend of the road.

LET NOT YOUR HEARTS
BE TROUBLED
John, Ch. 14

THE MYSTERY OF FAITH

**"Your hearts should no longer be troubled!
Believe in God,
believe also in me."**
The Lord's command comes after his prediction of
the soon-coming betrayal, denial, and separation.

He gives this command just when the scandal of scan-
dals is to break out: the putting to death of perfect Inno-
cence.

What are all the world's trials, all the world's injus-
tices compared to this?

When absurd death troubles our faith, when failure
shakes our confidence, when loneliness that only God can
know takes possession of our soul, all we have to do is to
repeat these words:

**"Your hearts should no longer be troubled,
believe in God,
believe also in me."**

This is not a blind faith—the kind of faith that would close its eyes to everything in life that seems absurd, inconsistent, a denial of God. On the contrary, it means facing up to all of this. And believing just the same, because of Jesus Christ and his cross.

The cross, paradoxical sign of a love stronger than denial and death; of defeat changed to victory.

God planted it at the center of the world so that all our contradictions may be solved in it.

Love and justice perpetually crucified by the world (this world of which I am a part), and only conquering the world by the cross.

Knowing that everything has a meaning, which we will know only at the end.

Clinging to that certainty.

"In my Father's house there are many places to dwell."

What do you mean, Lord? These words intrigue me. They are not meant only for Greeks and Judaists?

What vision did John have here?

And now I catch myself dreaming of all the treasures of humanity, of faith, of love, which will spread their glory in your Kingdom.

Families of souls with every one keeping its own originality, a prism glittering with unique light.

Barriers thrown down. All the riches of the nations, cultures, and human races transcended, integrated into the kingdom of light.

Vision of faith. The life of the Kingdom is still the unthinkable secret of God.

It is enough to think that the dwelling places are prepared, and our place is marked.

110

And we will be with him—in his service—forever.
Many dwellings, only one Way.

"I am the Way, the Truth and the Life."

A way is made to be followed. And our way is to
walk day after day in the Lord's footprints; to listen, to
obey, to allow ourselves to be led.

Then we will know *who he is.* And, through him, we
will know the Father.

Jesus Christ, the only Way leading to the *Father.*

"I am the Truth."

Jesus, truth lived out.

Far from an abstract truth, far from an intellectual
speculation of the kind relished by the Gnostics.

Truth, here, is a synonym of reality.

The reality of God, the reality of man, the reality of
things, all revealed in one life. In the down-to-earth
existence of a Palestinian Jew.

Jesus Christ: he in whom everything is "true," as God
is "true." His love is true, his faithfulness is true, his
holiness is true, his justice is true.

And, as a man, his obedience is true. His will is identi-
cal with his Father's. Total, voluntary submission.

Jesus, truth lived out.

Truth that can alone give meaning to my life. I may
sometimes doubt God. Not the truth of that life.

And because he believed, I believe.

"I am the Life."

The unique power vested in this life *to communicate
itself.* To give us an existence.

To liberate slaves; to resurrect the dead:

and we are those slaves;
we are the dead.

Seed of life eternal which already, in the depths of our being, is bringing forth its fruit of grace, peace, and joy.
Life unceasingly communicated:
by his word;
by his sacrament.
Life which must unceasingly be received anew if it is to be given. But also unceasingly given if it is to be received.
"Lord, show us the Father and we shall be satisfied."
Is Philip asking for another theophany such as those related in the Old Testament? Who is there who does not desire proof of God's existence?
No other will be given than *Jesus Christ.*

Jesus astonished: you have lived with me, and *yet you do not know me!*
He is not speaking of a carnal knowledge but of that discernment in faith which discovers, behind appearances, the mystery of the person, his origin and calling.
In order for Philip "to see" the Father in the Son, there must intervene the cross, the resurrection, and the coming of the Spirit. Then the mystery of the Servant, of the Ebed Yahweh, will be unveiled to his understanding and he will confess it with authority. (Acts 8:26–40.)

God unknowable without Jesus Christ.
But also, Jesus Christ inconceivable without the Father? For every one of his acts, every one of his words are submitted to God, placed under his unique and
112

sovereign authority. The unity of the Father and of the Son untiringly proclaimed.

Some of our contemporaries would prefer to do away with this concept of the Father—this childish myth. Paternalism is going through hard times. "Adult" man wants nothing to do with it. The word seems to have a strange, bad taste that is vaguely Freudian.

This brutal reality must therefore be faced unflinchingly: he who rejects the Father does not know the Son. Even worse: he rejects the Bible, entirely founded on faith in the Living God, on a direct and personal relationship between the Creator and the creature, on God's intervention—as a saving God—in the history of mankind.

Jesus not only believes and lives this relationship in a very unique way. He gives it an intimacy never before conceived. Whereas the Jews regard the name as so sacred they do not even pronounce it, Jesus chooses to use in speaking of God the most intimate and the most familiar of words, the word most naturally on the lips of every child: "**ABBA.**"

PRAYER IN JESUS' NAME

**"Amen, amen, I say to you,
he who believes in me
will also do
the works that I do.
He will do greater works,
because I am going to the Father."**
Jesus' earthly life is limited to space and time.
The power of the resurrected Jesus has no other

113

limits than those forced upon it by our unbelief.

We do not believe his promise and we hide our doubt under a mask of humility.

The apostles believed this word; they did the works of the Lord in the Holy Spirit's power.

And the gospel spread, irresistibly, in a world just as hostile to its message—let us make no mistake there— as our world of today.

"Whatever you ask in my name, I will do it."
We must meditate on the absoluteness of this promise. Asking "in Jesus' name" supposes that our will is in conformity with his. Then, and then only, is an answer sure.

"If you love me . . ." Obedience. Touchstone of our love; we are ever reminded of it.

THE PROMISED SPIRIT

The **"Paraclete"**: Intercessor, Counselor, Defender, and Upholder. "Spirit of Truth" given to the church to confirm her in faith.

He is promised to the disciples gathered together. The Lord's presence among his own, which differentiates the church from any other human grouping.

When this is recorded by the Gospel writer, this presence, this life-giving power is already living reality, glorious certainty, anticipation of the Parousia.

The disciples, orphans for a time, have been consoled by the Holy Spirit.

Henceforth they know *who* Jesus is. And that he is in the Father, and the Father in him.

And that the Son is in them, and they in him.

114

It is no undefinable mystical union, but a unity founded on faithful obedience; on a communion of will and of love.

"Lord, how is it that you manifest yourself to us, and not to the world?"

The disciples would like the Lord to manifest himself visibly, in a material way, to force the world to believe in him. But his incognito will continue on even after the resurrection. And only those will *recognize* him and receive him who have believed and loved him in his humiliation; those who have guarded his words.

Jesus Christ incognito. Still difficult to accept in our day.

Christ present in the world, but not recognized.

Present in the church, but often disregarded. Burlesqued.

Believers' privileges can become their condemnation. Because they consist in revealed grace and love which must be received, lived, communicated. And all this only for the service of others.

The Spirit's role is to continue the Son's work among his own, so they may in turn be "witnesses."

The Spirit sent *by the Father, in the Son's name.* Whose work is to engrave in our hearts what was said and done once and for all. And to enlighten its meaning from one generation to another.

The church taught by the Holy Spirit. Brought back by him, through all the vicissitudes of flesh and spirit, to her origin and center.

The Spirit invents nothing. He is Witness to the Son,

115

as the Son is Witness to the Father. But he enlightens the church, from age to age, concerning the meaning of his Coming; he opens up for her endless horizons. He reveals old things and makes them new.

THE GIFT OF PEACE

**"I leave with you peace;
I give you my peace;
not as the world gives
do I give to you."**
Ancient greeting of the Semitic peoples: "shalom"; "salaam."
Health, harmony, integrity of the being.
Peace coming down, a promise and a prayer, on every house visited. But it can be refused. (Luke 10:5–6.)

"My peace."
Communion of the Son with the Father, that nothing henceforth will be able to trouble.
The peace brought by him is reconciliation with God and reconciliation with men.
The restoration of lost communion.

This peace is promised by Jesus just when all the splits and clashes are coming to a head.
The hour of failure and abandonment.
Peace given as his last testament to those he is leaving. To those who in a moment will be fleeing and denying him.
The last words of the condemned Man.
The first words of the resurrected One.
Peace that the world knows not.

Peace that is not security, neither is it quiet. It is not a state of the soul. But his peace who obeyed in all things, who keeps us strong and tranquil at the heart of the battle.

The disciples will only understand all this later on.
Someday they will experience obedience unto death. Then they will know.

"The prince of this world is coming.
He has no power over me."
Jesus is not minimizing Satan's power, the reality of his hold on the man of this world.
But he is simply stating that Satan **"has nothing in him."**
The mystery of Jesus Christ: he is *intact*. No external force can break through his armor. This is where his divinity breaks through.

In each of us there are strongholds of secret complicity where the enemy knows how to attack and conquer us. That is why we have no other recourse than the victory won by Jesus Christ.

THE TRUE VINE
John, Chs. 15; 16:1–4

THE VINE AND THE BRANCHES

"I am the true vine,
and my Father is the vinedresser."
The long patience of the vinedresser.
How many million years, Lord, before this earth was ready?
ready one day to bring forth your fruit?

Israel, beloved vine, chosen by you, planted by you.
Judah, chosen plant, jealously kept. (Isa. 5:1–6; cf.
Ps. 80:8–19.)

Moses, David, the prophets. They all spaded, planted,
pruned, cut back, replanted in your name.
Wild bunches. Sour juice.
The holy anger of flouted love.
How many centuries of effort, how many crop failures,
O God our Father,
Before the true Vine was placed in the earth by you?

Nourishing sap climbing from the stem to the
branches

to carry there its fruit of grace and truth.
Your blood, your given life.

But dry branches exist, also. Good for the fire.
And all the branches must be pruned.
Pruning of the vine—bleeding under the vinedresser's knife.
The vine must bleed for the fruit to be beautiful.

Your liberating word has rung out in our ears.
All we must do now is to let you act.
And receive all from your grace,
from day to day.
But this is exactly what my vanity does not want.

Poor sour grapes where the ego slipped in,
wormy fruit with a divided heart.
Cut, Lord! Cut them off and burn them!
and may only your fruit be left!
My present balky life must stop:
one day I give myself to you, the next I want myself back again.
You must reign at last in our hearts and minds.
Living in you. Receiving you in ourselves.
The word, the sacrament—life-giving sap. Wine of Life.
Food ever new and always given afresh.
Food that must become blood of our blood, flesh of our flesh.

There is no such thing as an independent branch—
unless it is the one already cut off; good for the fire.
The sap climbs from a single trunk. You want your church, as a mighty tree,

to spread out her branches.
You want the beauty of her fruit to attract the passing travelers.
Heavy bunches full of juice,
the wine of joy, of peace, of charity,
the wine of your given life.
Given for the entire world.

**"By this my Father is glorified,
that you bear much fruit,
and so show yourselves my disciples."**
The tree judged according to its fruit.
Faith produces fruits of love as surely as a healthy vine produces grapes.
Progression from the Father to the Son, from the Son to the disciples, from the disciples to those whom God places in their pathway.

**"Greater love has no man than this,
that a man lay down his life for his friends."**
The church, mystery of love; a love drawn from the very heart of the divine Trinity, drawing its members together with indissoluble bonds.
Unconditional love, merciful love, love that will not hesitate, if necessary, to give its own life.

What would the influence of our parishes be if we lived this out?
What drawing power for the surrounding world, so poor in true love.
How difficult it is, Lord, to love our brothers. They sit in the same pews with us, but we do not even know them.

"You are my friends."

The friend has no less responsibility to obey than the servant. But the friend's outward life becomes communion of faith and hope. He enters into his Lord's plans, and accords them all the strength of his being.

"Friend of God." That is said in the Old Testament, as far as I know, only of Abraham and Moses.

Abraham—believed God's promises to the point of giving his only son.

Moses—God's confidant who carried out his plans for the people;

the man who **"considered abuse suffered for Christ greater wealth than the treasures of Egypt."**

"You did not choose me."

The disciples were set apart, "chosen" for a unique ministry as *witnesses*. Safekeepers of their Master's most intimate thoughts. Called to know **"the power of his resurrection and to share in his sufferings"** (Phil. 3:10).

But beyond the disciples these words of Jesus are valid for all those whom he calls to serve him. There is no genuine vocation that does not carry his seal.

What expressive grace!—his hand resting on our shoulder for time and eternity. Our only security.

But this grace is accompanied by a requirement: to bring forth fruit, a fruit **"that abides."** And this fruit is brotherly service, in the unity of love.

THE WORLD AND ITS HATE

**"If the world hates you,
know that it has hated me before it hated you."**

A certain identity of destiny necessarily exists between the master and his disciples.

Those who believed his Word will also believe theirs.

Those who rejected him will also reject them.

Jesus is preparing his disciples for the scandal of his own rejection so they may not lose heart.

But also for their own trials—for the lot that is soon to be theirs.

The church yet young soon knew hate and persecution. She received the baptism of blood.

She conquered the pagan world not by power but by martyrdom.

The age of Constantine: temporal and spiritual power united by a pact of coexistence. Each hoping to dominate the other.

The world ensconced in the church, the church ensconced in the world. Strengthening each other.

And now a new era begins. The pact is broken. The world is no longer linked to the church.

The institution is challenged. It is no longer untouchable and sacred.

Rather, fragile and threatened.

Why do you wonder, church of Jesus Christ, at coming back to your true condition again?

It is when the great men of this earth flatter you and honor you that you should start trembling.

But when they recognize in you the impregnable bastion of faith, against which all totalitarianism is to be shattered,

all ideologies exhausted,

then rejoice.

Your Lord is with you.
But beware lest this world's attack
should turn against you.
For it often hates you both for what you are,
and for what you are not.
For this hostile world, without being aware of it, is
looking toward you
for the justice, truth, and genuineness which it has
not yet found in you.

Blessed are you, feeble, denuded church,
living from the grace of the crucified Christ only.

"They hate me without cause." (Ps. 35:19; 69:4.)
Jesus takes for himself the cry of the Righteous Man
in the psalms; the cry of righteous men of all time;
for in him their destiny is fulfilled.

For his witnesses of all time he promises the Spirit's
assistance—and persecution.

"I HAVE OVERCOME THE WORLD"
John 16:5–33

THE COMING OF THE PARACLETE

"Where are you going?"
The question is burning on the disciples' lips, but no one dares express it.

Jesus still present but already far away.

The chasm made by death's approach between those who stay on and the one who is leaving. His eyes are turned elsewhere.

The disciples see only the soon-coming separation, and the great, threatening unknown.

Jesus sees the final result: his work completed, his return to the Father, the gift of the Spirit.

The Lord's departure, condition for the Paraclete's coming. He is the Counselor, the Witness: Jesus' new way of being with his own.
**"And when he comes
he will convince the world
of sin
of righteousness
of judgment."**

There is no other real "sin" than the refusal of the Living God; of his proffered grace, manifested in the gift he gave us of his Son.

Thus the cross lays bare, in its natural state, the "hate for God" residing in man's heart; his first rebellion, his permanent rebellion, this continual ruin which he refuses to recognize.

God's justice breaks forth in the enthronement of his crucified Son.

A double trial, a double judgment are to unfold on the earth and in heaven.

He who is condemned by men is justified by God and raised up to his right hand.

The accuser, the prince of this world, is cast out from God's presence, reduced to silence.

He who was crucified, conqueror over all the powers of hate and death, is henceforth our surety and defender at God's throne.

"I have yet many things to say to you,
but you cannot bear them now."
Jesus knows the day will come when his apostles will grasp the meaning of his words and acts.

Patience of God—he knows how to wait for his hour. The disciples have heard Jesus. They have seen him at work. But nevertheless they still have not understood him. For them to grasp the meaning of his mission, the cross and the resurrection must do their work. And the Holy Spirit.

"When the Spirit of truth comes
he will guide you into all truth."
Jesus promised his disciples that the Spirit would
125

reveal to them the fullness of all truth regarding him. This is the basis of their unique authority.

We must therefore believe their testimony, humbly, even when it is beyond our understanding. For it is on the testimony that the Lord was pleased to build his church, and it is our only recourse through all the controversies of the centuries.

But the church, marching toward her Lord, led by the Spirit, will herself grasp only slowly all that is virtually contained in this original testimony; for this can never be assimilated except by those who receive it and live in its grace and in its demands. It will not be received in its fullness except in the communion of the saints.

In the one church: one in truth and in love.

"I have yet many things to say to you." Jesus is saying this to each and to all.

Like Isaiah, all we yet see are the edges of his robe of glory. (Isa., ch. 6.) And already we think we have known and experienced? already we are strong?

But this robe of glory was sufficient for the prophet to realize himself a sinner; for him to receive forgiveness and the grace of a call from God.

Obscurity and contradictions of the gospel. The Lord of Glory represented as a humble servant.

Yes, it is true **"no one can say, 'Jesus is Lord' except by the Holy Spirit"** (I Cor. 12:3).

The Spirit, Witness, and Creator of life. Present when the world was created. At the incarnation. At the birth of the church; at the baptism which makes us a part of her. Mysterious agent of the future world at work in the world of today.

126

DEPARTURE AND RETURN

**"A little while and you will see me no more,
again a little while and you will see me."**
To which return is he referring? His appearance after
the resurrection? the gift of the Spirit? the Parousia?
Certainly all of these at once.

After the disciples' confusion, the world's mocking,
will come the appearance of the resurrected Christ, the
joy of his victory sealed in willing hearts by the Spirit.
But that coming is only the promise of another
coming: his glorious Advent.
The church lives in this hope, she lives this hope.
The pain of childbirth.
On Calvary, Jesus Christ gave birth to the church.
And the church in turn gives birth in pain.
Spiritual birth is exactly like physical birth: it costs
something.
But great is the joy when the child is born: a man
born to eternal life.

The long labor of the world's birth. Continuing with
its anguish, its troubles, and its joys until the final consummation, until that day known only of God when
he will be **"all in all."**
Then all will be fullness of joy.
Then all the impenetrable mysteries of this life will
be explained.
We cannot, finite creatures that we are, speak of the
things of God without figures and symbols. That is why
Jesus speaks to us in parables. But the time is coming
when we will know as we have been known.

"At last you are speaking clearly!" . . . "Now we believe."

What an illusion!

Tomorrow they will doubt. Tomorrow they will lose heart.

We have no right to be sure of anything—except of *GOD'S faithfulness.*

"The hour is coming, indeed it has come,
when you will be scattered every man his own way,
and will leave me alone."

Jesus, even before his hour strikes, knows he will be totally abandoned by men—

by his nearest friends, his dearest companions—

but also totally in his Father's hand.

Jesus suffers all possible loneliness, so as to be with us in ours.

"I have said this to you,
that in me you may have peace.
In the world you will have to suffer.
But keep up your courage!
I have overcome the world."

Believe this victory. Live under its banner: such is the entire gospel.

Lord, your victory has been proclaimed for nineteen centuries now, and the world has not changed much.

Willful powers running rampant as never before. Money powers. Powers of destruction. All the demons of hell in league.

Was your victory only a delusion?

No.

128

You warned your disciples of the coming struggles. And that the assaults would be even stronger at the end of time.

Of course there are days when doubt assails us.

But nevertheless we know, with an intimate and profound certainty, that we belong to you.

Your grace and your forgiveness have made their way into our lives. Divine guarantees of our liberation. Humble surety of the world's salvation.

The church was brought forth with songs of thanksgiving; sung by those who were **"more than conquerors"** (Rom. 8:37) through him who loved them. Men who knew your joy and your peace.

Lord, in this tired, disillusioned world, make your Christians witnesses of this victory, of this peace.

Give us your tonic of joy.

CONSECRATION
John, Ch. 17

"Father, the hour has come:
Glorify your Son,
so that your Son may glorify you,
and since you have given him power over all flesh,
may he give eternal life
to all whom you have given him."

"Father, the hour has come."
The hour he has for so long awaited.
Feared.
Desired.

Glory of redeeming love.
Glory of the Father revealed in the Son.
Glory of the Son offered to the Father.
Glory of the harvest of men
whom the Father gives to his Son,
whom the Son brings to his Father.
Living, Lord, is entering into this mystery of love.
Is knowing you as him who gives himself unceasingly,
unlimitedly, for the salvation of men.

**"I have glorified you on earth;
I have completed the work
you gave me
to do."**

Oh, Lord! This work has barely begun!

A few blind who see, a few crippled who walk, what is that?

How many have seen your earthly steps?

How many believe?

Look at your poor humanity, after twenty centuries, still suffering blindness?

and still pitiless?

Three years' ministry finished on a cross.

Lord, help us believe that what you did there
has really changed the face of the world,
for it is hard to see.

Help us, whatever may happen, to believe your victory.

Yes, your work is complete;
your flesh is given, your blood poured out.
The eternal seed is sown.
The hour of your witnesses is about to strike.
Those whom the Father himself has chosen and given;
those whom the Son has instructed and prepared.
Such a feeble and fragile beginning.
Predestined beginning.

The Son's faith in these feeble disciples,
because they were chosen, given,
by his offering sanctified.
The church is planted at the very heart of the world,
mystery of faith,

mystery of frailty,
dwelling place of the Holy Spirit
belied by carnal man.

Your glory, Lord, was hidden in your incarnation.

How much more difficult will it be to believe its presence tomorrow,

in this new temple whose foundations you are now laying,

in this body nourished with your flesh and blood?

PRAYER FOR HIS MESSENGERS

**"I am praying for them;
I am not praying for the world,
but for those you have given me,
for they are yours."**

Are these words not difficult, Lord? These are the "called," who must be prayed for and struggled for? Those upon whom the Father has set his seal? And then . . . there are all the rest, the noncalled? Those whose hour has not yet arrived—that hour which it would be vain to try to move up?

Who is the "world" here, Lord? The masses who do not know you, or those who have deliberately refused to know you?

But it is still the world you loved. It is this whole world that your Son came to save.

But from now on the world can only know the mystery of your love through those who "know," chosen from the beginning, predestined witnesses of the resurrection.

The Son is imploring your grace on these few,
now when the separation of death is imminent.
They are the firstfruits of the great harvest.
They are the ones upon whom everything depends,
now.
Heralds of the finished work,
confessors of the Word made flesh,
the newborn of the Spirit.

The unique role of the Lord's apostles.
He concentrates his prayer on them.
The Spirit's flame comes down on them.
Guardians of the faith throughout all ages,
who must be believed and reverenced.

Men, yes. Weak men.
But sent out by the Lord himself:
"As you sent me, so I am sending them."
Such a sovereign delegation of authority as to make us
tremble.
Mysterious transfer from the Father to the Son,
from the Son to the disciples.
Transfer of power and of love.

This is the church's trust, her cross and her joy:
to guard this entrusted faith.
Proclaimed faith. Faith lived out. Its substance nourishing the whole world.
Yes, how could the Lord not entreat his Father
"to keep" his own?
Kept by the Father. Kept by the Spirit,
at the final hour
when he is to leave them?

133

Keep us, Lord. We also need to be kept.
In the hour of temptation, in the hour of death,
when night is creeping over our hearts.

And now, Lord, the memory of those with
whom you entrusted me is burning in my heart.
Those I was unable to "keep."
Have pity on them, have pity on me, Lord.
How frail our faith, how frail our prayers.
Only you can "keep" your own. But you, even you,
you were unable to "keep" Judas.
Mystery of human liberty, of such a terrible power of
refusal. Refusal so often final.
Were you not lifted up, Lord, on a cross,
to draw, someday, all men to you?
Even men like Caiaphas, like Judas?
How could we ever enter into that fullness of joy
which is yours and which you want to be ours,
if such were not the case?

All our resistance consumed
in the great fire of your love.
Fullness of pardon, fullness of love, fullness of joy,
fullness of life received and given,
fullness of communion experienced again.

Lord, when the battle is at its worst, yourself on the
threshold of agony,
you speak to us of victory and of joy.
There is in you no flight to another world,
but a certainty of faith
that nothing is lost, nothing is hopeless,
if *God is*.

Communion of suffering. Martyrs' joy,
giving their lives lovingly for you.

Perhaps because we have never learned to suffer with you,
we hardly know anymore, Lord, what is meant by
your joy.

"They are not of the world,
even as I am not of the world.
Sanctify them in the truth:
your word is truth.
As you sent me into the world,
so I have sent them into the world."
Trying to live "in" the world, without being "of" the
world, that, Lord, is just our problem.
For the world is in us and has no trouble taking rapid
possession of us.

You want no part of our escaping and hiding.
Escape into the well-meaning ghetto of the "saved."
Escape into dreaming.
Escape into piousness.
Escape from a world asking us too many questions;
from a world where the communist and the atheist
are looking honestly, rigorously, for their truth;
from a world of hunger, misery, and promiscuity;
from a world where revolt rumbles on, and blasphemy,
because we have not loved it.

Lord, to know what it means to be in the world but
not of the world, we must look to you.
To you, so near to every man, to every woman we may
meet. To you, for whom nothing human is foreign. To
you, friend of Samaritans and tax gatherers.

To you who were free with such a marvelous freedom.
Free of every uneasiness and every prejudice.

But still, Lord, so visibly "from somewhere else." In this very nearness, in this very freedom, "Other" than all the others, than all those who are of the earth.

Other because you are true. As God only is true.

Authenticity of every word, of every act.
Lord, make us more human. And truer.
You want us in this world, thoroughly involved in it.
Sharing in its joys and pains.

But with the mark on the forehead, the cross of the redeemed, the wound in the heart that you impose on all whom you love.

Deeply rooted by our Baptism, by our Communion,
by your word of truth believed and meditated,
in another life, another Reality.

But here we are, in spite of ourselves, often
"far off and different."
And for the world, bothersome.

Send us into the world, Lord.
Fill us with the burning fire of your love.
But may we at all times and places
be yours.

THAT THEY MAY BE ONE . . .

"I do not pray for these only."
Now, Lord, your prayer goes beyond your
apostles to take in those who will hear them,

136

believers of all ages.
Us, the latecomers in the harvest.
Sovereign intercession of the crucified Christ,
the seal forever set by his offering.
Sovereign intercession of the resurrected Christ,
who reigns at God's right hand.

Grant us, Lord, to believe it, and to live from it;
to lean on it
when our weak faith stumbles;
and to raise our eternal thanksgiving to you
for your vigilant love.

Keep and save your church, Lord,
by the all-powerfulness of your prayer.
Keep her in love and in truth.

"May they all be one.
Even as you, Father, are in me,
and I in you,
may they also be one in us,
so that the world may believe
that you have sent me."
Unity of Father and Son, unfathomable mystery.
How could we, Lord, ever search it out?
But you want it to live in earthly substance,
in obedience every day renewed.
The unity that you ask us to reflect
is unity
of will,
of purpose,
of love.
All that the Father desires, the Son desires,
in the same way.

All that the Father does, the Son does,
in the same way.
**"My food is to do the will of my Father and to
accomplish his work."**
And this work is the salvation of the world.

Entering into the communion of the Father and Son
is doing their will,
is desiring what they desire,
is loving with their love.
It is serving this magnificent, terrible world they
created;
this lost world they have not ceased loving;
this dead world they want to resurrect,
to awaken to justice and truth.

Entering into the communion of the Father and Son
is being, at the center of a world torn apart,
miraculously healed by love and pardon,
the family of reconciled sinners.
It is being the sign an old world is waiting for,
of a new world, a redeemed world,
of a brotherly, free world—free with the glorious
freedom of God's children.

The grace of Pentecost:
"They were all one—one in heart and soul."
But how short, Lord, this moment was.

The evil one is watching. He cannot destroy the work
accomplished.
His sport will be to divide what you united.

But you did not neglect telling us: it is by the love

we have for each other that the world will know of your Coming.

The conclusive sign it is asking for—that it has a right to expect—is the unity of the believers.

That new society where all ostracism has disappeared; where money, race, caste, no longer count.

Because all live from the same grace, from the same pardon.

Lord, take a look at our parishes. Look at your poor Christians: sometimes harder, colder, less open than the surrounding world.

Strange self-righteousness which always comes back: mortal danger run up against by "religious people" of all ages. They are the ones who set up your cross. They are the ones who yet today are trying to mask it over.

Crucified love, trying from high on a cross to draw all men to him.

You wanted us to love our brothers with that kind of love.

The humble love of one reprieved man for another.

Lord, look at the history of your church: her violence, all those she has burned at the stake.

All the violence, all the domineering, all the exploiting of the weak by the strong she has tolerated, justified.

Is it astonishing that those who were exploited yesterday should remember it? That they judge us and condemn us?

Lord, all this you know. You knew it all when, about to die, you were giving your final warnings.

You knew it, you know it, and you do not abandon us.

And your Spirit is always blowing afresh on the old, dry bones and giving them life.

He is blowing today, Lord. Who would dare deny it?

Breath of repentance and renewal, which is shaking your whole church.

For the first time, in twenty centuries, your church is weeping over her divisions, and accusing herself.

And rethinking her mission to the world today.

Wake us up, Lord, while there is still time.

Help us to lay hold of the hour you give us.

Perhaps the last before the night?

GLORY TO COME

"Father,
I desire
that they also whom you have given me
may be with me,
where I am,
to behold my glory
that you have given me
because you loved me
before the creation of the world."

Someday, we will see. Someday, we will know **"as we have been known."**

All veils will be torn apart which still hide his face and his love.

"Beloved,
we are God's children now;
it does not yet appear what we shall be,
but we know that when he appears,
we shall be like him,
for we shall see him as he is." (I John 3:2.)

Like you, Lord! Transfigured by your all-powerful love.

Infinite glory of the Son, reflected in his own.
Mysterious conformation, work of the Holy Spirit.

You want nothing less than this, Lord: to have us
with you, where you will be,
   near to your Father's heart.

These words make me dizzy, Lord. They are too great
for me.
   But there is one thing I know. This glory,
   which you call upon us to contemplate,
   was, is, will be, for all eternity,
   the glory of the sacrificed Lamb.
   A mystery of life offered and given.
   This mystery, revealed to your apostles,
   is what we must believe, live, and proclaim.

JESUS AT THE MERCY OF MAN
John 18:1 to 19:16

SHOULD I NOT DRINK OF THIS CUP?

Jesus crosses the brook Kidron, seeking seclusion one last time in the Garden.

A guard mobilized to take him who offers no defense.

Jesus handed over, betrayed. In truth, handing himself over, knowing his hour has come: **"Shall I not drink the cup which the Father has given me?"**

Jesus master of his destiny, even now.

God present but hidden, directing all.

Unbeknown to the guards, and to Judas, and to Caiaphas,

and to the disciples themselves.

Men easily think themselves masters over events. Far from it.

Through them, in spite of them, today as at that time, God is directing the world toward the end marked out by himself.

Peter's untimely zeal.

In spite of the Lord's warning, how many Christians throughout history have thought it necessary to defend their faith with the sword?

142

Miserable Christianity, not yet to have understood that truth is defended by shedding one's own blood, not someone else's.

JESUS BEFORE ANNAS AND CAIAPHAS

Jesus tied up like a criminal.

Jesus led first before Annas then before Caiaphas: their prestige is not any too much to condemn an innocent man.

A mockery of an interrogation. The verdict is obtained. This man must die **"for the people."**

For the security of the established institution . . .

Yes, Lord, you are a dangerous man. Many things will disappear because you decided to come into the world. Caiaphas' fear was justified.

And now he is doing God's work. Only hastening what he wanted to keep from happening. Unawares he seals his people's fate.

Jesus gives no answer to Annas' questions but unmasks their hypocrisy. His teaching has been done publicly. In broad daylight no one had dared to arrest him.

Only two disciples follow the prisoner. One is known and has no trouble entering; perhaps the author of this Gospel? The other, Simon, is only able to enter because he is a friend of the first. This is clearly in the text.

It seems strange that the four Gospel writers should be so careful to tell us of Peter's denial. As though they wanted to emphasize his frailty, and that his authority as leader of the apostles is pure grace, nothing else.

Thus the church has shown us, from her beginning, everything is founded on grace and pardon.

John tells us nothing of Jesus' interrogation before Caiaphas. He has given us elements indicating the basic issue of the trial ever since the beginning of his Gospel. When he is writing, the important thing is the church's relationship with Roman authority. It must be shown that Pilate recognized Jesus to be innocent, and only crucified him because of pressure from the Jewish authorities.

We read that the Jews do not enter the praetorium **"so that they might not be defiled, but might eat the passover."** Not afraid of defiling themselves with a murder, but afraid of defiling themselves by crossing the threshold of a Gentile building. Rites are more important than a man's life.

Let us not accuse the Jews. A lot of people have been killed in the name of religion. A false zeal that ignores divine and human reality has always existed.

Pilate meets Jesus' detractors halfway. Religious quarrels are of no interest to him. What he wants is to get rid of the whole affair. But the Jewish authorities insist on an official condemnation. His punishment must be that of the cross; then everyone will know that he was a false messiah, cursed of God, for:
"Cursed be anyone hung on a tree" (Deut. 21:23; cf. Gal. 3:13).

Thus, the Gospel writer tells us, his predicted destiny comes to pass.

144

TWO KINGDOMS MEET

"Are you the king of the Jews?"
—"My kingdom is not of this world."
Mysterious incognito of his royalty. Incognito till the end of time.

For your arms, Lord, are not the world's arms, and the world does not recognize them.

Any seeking after temporal power, any recourse to the arms of the world betray his royalty.

The church has often forgotten that truth: she has wanted to be victorious and not crucified.

Someday, all the kingdoms of this world will collapse, and your royalty will be revealed with the glory of a blinding flash of lightning.

All our lies will be consumed in the fire of your holiness. Our illusions destroyed. Our self-importance blotted out.

Mystery of this King who wants to be abased; suffering, crucified, and can—and wants—to draw all men to him only from high on a cross.

The only place where all our human wisdom, all our selfishness and pride can come and be broken.

All-powerfulness of redeeming love. Stronger than all the world's strength. Stronger than death.

"What is truth?"
It is here before you, Pilate: incarnate in the weakness of this defenseless man who is about to die.

About to die for you, Pilate, Roman governor; for you and all the others:

for the small and for the great;

for the wise and for the powerful—those who think themselves wise—those who think themselves powerful.

145

Pilate is skeptical; but not indifferent to the authority emanating from this man. He cannot help feeling that he is the victim of some cabal, an innocent man. He tries to get himself out of the predicament by giving the crowd the choice of freeing Jesus or Barabbas.

—"Not this man, but Barabbas!"

The Holy One judged more dangerous than the criminal.

Jesus beaten, crowned with thorns. Clothed in royal purple. Slapped. Jeered.

Pilate, ill at ease, tries to put the blame of this denial of justice on other shoulders. Takes Jesus out of the praetorium.

"Here is the man!"

Yes, here is the man: you have not realized, Pilate, the depth of your own words.

Here is the man: poor king of creation, weak and ridiculous, clad in a purple robe and a thorny crown.

King unthroned, disfigured, sad likeness of failed destiny.

Here is the man: the Holy One, silent through beating and insults, taking on himself man's shame and disgrace before God.

"Crucify him." According to John the cry of "the chief priests and the officers"—spiritual guardians, temporal guardians of the establishment.

Pilate tries a third time to find a way out. Worried about justice? superstitious fear? if this man were really "the Son of God"?

"Where are you from?"

It is now the Roman magistrate's turn to ask this

146

question, asked by the crowd, the Pharisees, and the scribes throughout Christ's ministry.

Jesus is a mystery. His being is one continual question for men. But many, once it is asked, pass on.

Jesus is silent. For Pilate's question is not a question of faith.

"Don't you know?"

—"You would have no power over me unless it had been given you from above."

What could you do, Pilate, if Someone greater than you had not given you power over me?

You think you are master, and you are only an instrument. An unknowing instrument of a divine plan.

Jesus does not say that Pilate bears no guilt. He is guilty as a Roman magistrate, as an upholder of the law. But Jesus states very clearly that the sin of the religious leaders is greater before God. For in fact they are rejecting the God they claim as theirs, they are treating a lie as truth. And they show themselves thus to be sons of him who is by nature a *liar* and a *murderer*. (Cf. John, ch. 8.)

"We have no king but Caesar!"

Now not only Jesus is rejected, but the whole Jewish identity as such is denied by the high priest.

The King rejected here is God himself.

Reasons of state have done their work. The procurator's future is at stake. It is best that Jesus die.

"Then he handed him over to them to be crucified."

Justice will be denied numerous times through the course of history. But the heaviest denials in eternal scales, perhaps the only which should make us tremble,

147

are those committed in God's name and in the name of his Christ. And they will be numerous.

Christians, let us not incriminate Caiaphas or Judas. Let us rather be silent before this mystery of blindness which, at times, strikes the church herself (or her representatives).

Perhaps, Lord, it was necessary for Jews and heathen to join in this crime in order for them to partake someday of the same pardon?

"God," according to Paul, "has consigned all men to disobedience, that he may have mercy upon all.

"O the depth of the riches and wisdom and knowledge of God! How unsearchable are his judgments and how inscrutable his ways!" (Rom. 11:32–33.)

CRUCIFIED
John 19:17–42

Jesus crucified. Not alone but between two thieves. Condemned for political reasons, but reduced to the level of a common criminal; sharing the lot of those the world has despised most.

So that henceforth no one be excluded from his mysterious fellowship.

"Jesus of Nazareth, king of the Jews."
Written in three languages to be sure that everyone understands. Poltical act whose derisive meaning the Jewish authorities catch only too well. Pilate, once more the instrument of the divine plan—what he has today proclaimed for everyone to see will be an article of faith for tomorrow's church.

The murder does not bother the high priest's conscience, only the sign.

Lots are cast for the Lord's seamless tunic. It is marred by no tears.

We Christians have torn it. History has seen the unique robe of royal priesthood cut into pieces by our divisions.

149

The Fourth Gospel only mentions Mary twice: at the Cana wedding and at the foot of the cross.

The Mother's slow agony is her secret: only God can measure its depth and weigh her struggles.

All the hidden pain mothers know was symbolically borne in *this* mother's pain.

Jesus entrusts his mother to the disciple he loves, and the disciple to his mother.

Thus Mary, at the height of her Calvary experience, obtains the grace of being a mother again.

"I am thirsty."
"I looked for pity, but there was none,
And for comforters, but I found none.
They gave me poison for food,
And for my thirst they gave me vinegar to drink."
(Ps. 69:20–21.)

The agonizing cries of the psalms—announcing and foreshadowing this unique agony which is to take in all others.

Thirst: the crucified Christ's greatest torment. The vinegar was supposed to relieve his thirst. One act of pity from the soldiers.

He who is the fountain of living water in an agony of thirst. At the mercy of a Roman soldier.

Physical thirst.

Thirst of the Holy One bearing in himself all men's thirsting, all men's hopes.

All the world's thirst endured, quenched by him.

Church of Jesus Christ, entrusted with his living water, do you consider men's thirst as something really serious?

Thirst for water, yes, pure drinkable water.

Thirst for life.

Thirst for love.

Thirst for justice.

Thirst for truth.

"It is finished."

The Son's work on earth is done.

"He bowed his head and gave up his spirit."

THE SPEAR

Jesus, the real paschal lamb. All the sacrifices throughout the ages were only figures of him.

It is right that none of his bones be broken.

It is right that his blood flow—be spilled—to give life to the world.

Blood of the covenant, living water of the Spirit.

Jesus' baptism—baptism of water and of blood.

Given life.

"This is he who came

by water and blood, Jesus Christ,

not with water only

but with water and blood." (I John 5:6.)

"They will look upon him whom they pierced."

"And I will pour out on the house of David and the inhabitants of Jerusalem

a spirit of compassion and supplication,

and they shall look on him whom they pierced.
They shall mourn for him as for an only child;
they shall weep bitterly over him, as one weeps over
a firstborn." (Zech. 12:10.)
—"What are these wounds in your hands?
—These wounds I received in the house of my
friends." (Zech. 13:6.)
Many people have been crucified in this world.
What is unique about this cross is the One nailed upon
it.
To break our hard hearts and make them cry
a God had to be crucified.

Lies crucifying truth.
Hate crucifying love.
The unbearable part of holiness.
And God looking down, from high on that cross,
unmasking it all.
Contemplate the cross. Feel his look condemning and
liberating—
a look that pierces through to the unimagined depths
of my being.
Mystery of forgiveness, of grace, of life.

Lord, give us the courage to contemplate you,
to let you look upon us
until your look unmasks us, sparing nothing;
until your grace and your peace descend on us;

until the great mystery of life as an absolute gift
opens to us.

THE BURIAL

No one of the disciples who followed Jesus openly now dares to ask Pilate for the body of their crucified Master, only Joseph of Arimathea, "a disciple of Jesus, but secretly."

And Nicodemus, who could not bring himself to serve the living Christ, brings one hundred pounds of myrrh and aloes for his burial.

Human beings thus find an alibi and a consolation in honoring cadavers.

HE LIVES
John, Ch. 20

"They have taken away my Lord."

Mary of Magdala: out of whom Jesus cast seven devils (Luke 8:2): one of the humble Galilean women who followed him all the way to Calvary.

Mary of Magdala, the first at the tomb.

"They have taken the Lord out of the tomb, and we do not know where they have laid him."

Heartfelt cry.

Why, Mary—you who believed in him—
why are you shown to us this morning,
full of doubt and anguish before the empty tomb?

The sundering power of death: the body which can no longer be touched, the eye forever closed.

Who, before this mystery, has never wavered?

What faith has never for an instant gone under?

The silence of death: the most terrible negation of God.

Let them at least respect his dead body!

Mary thought the body had been stolen.

The Jews, later, believed it and repeated it.

John knows this and will not hesitate to refute them.

154

Lord, could the multitudes today not cry out with Mary,

"They have taken away my Lord and I do not know where they have laid him"?

Do we not satiate their ears with statements that "GOD IS DEAD" and man emancipated?

Jesus comes near to Mary, but she takes him for the gardener. And only recognizes him when he speaks her name.

How full of meaning!

He reveals himself by his word.

Simon Peter and the beloved disciple have come on the run. The beloved disciple runs faster but enters the last. **"He saw and believed."**

The linen cloths and the napkin are in perfect order: the body could not have been stolen.

But the tangible proofs are valid evidence only for the one already touched by grace.

THE EVENING IN THE UPPER ROOM

The disciples have come together, **"all the doors being closed."**

They are afraid.

Then, Lord, is when you come.

You come through shut doors. One more mysterious appearance.

"Peace be with you." The standard greeting repeated by all Jews from time immemorial, so many times the Lord's.

This time it falls from the lips of the resurrected Lord.

And now it gently, sovereignly, descends on these fearful, helpless disciples.

You show them your hands and side.

The new body given to you is still your wounded body.

Marks of love nothing can efface.

"Peace be with you!" Mystery of pardon. Mystery of communion.

Peace that the world does not know and cannot give, for it flows from the side of the resurrected Christ.

"They were filled with joy."

Today you come, Lord, as you did then, through our shut doors.

And the sign of your coming is pardon, peace, joy.

It is being sent.

**"As the Father sent me,
so I am sending you."**

As the Father sent the Son and vested him with his authority, as the Son can say or do nothing which has not been given him, so the Son gives power to his apostles to speak and act in his name.

Finished. No more shut doors. The world must be reached.

This world God so loved
that he came to be crucified in it.

"And when he had said this, he breathed on them."

Reminder of God's creative breath on the first man.

A new humanity is about to be born,
begotten of the Holy Spirit.

For he only can make of these fallible apostles infallible witnesses of Truth.

156

He only can give them the extraordinary power of remitting sins
and of *retaining* them.
These words trouble us, Lord.
The judiciary power of the church has entailed so much misuse.
How many saints were suspected and condemned?
Easy absolution and refused grace . . . all this, Lord, is still very human.
Should your church not tremble
before the examination in thunder and lightning of the Last Judgment?

Grace of absolution which must be believed,
received, humbly, from your hand,
each time we hear it announced.
The Holy Spirit: mysterious and hidden power.
Spirit of discernment, Spirit of truth.
Power of love and lucidity.
Witness at the very heart of the church of the incarnate Word.
A wind **"blowing where it wants,"** a wind sweeping over the world and its history driving them toward their end,
the end God has desired.

THOMAS

"Unless I see in his hands the print of the nails . . ."
The man who wants "to see" to believe, who asks for tangible proof.
The man with a scientific bent. The strong mind only believing in "facts."

157

Only in material proof.
Show me your God and I'll believe in him!

Sometimes God does show himself, as here. And, in
his mercy, he gives us a visible sign of his presence.
But such is not faith's way.
**"Because you have seen me
you believe.
Blessed are those who will believe
without seeing."**
Those in whose ears the apostles' words will ring
from age to age.
And who, at that word, will give over their lives.
The Son's faith was naked obedience.
He calls us to the same obedience.

None of the signs the gospel gives us
have ever convinced anyone on the spot.
The disciples followed you without ever understanding
where you were leading them.
Then, when the time came,
they believed.
"My Lord and my God!"
Decisive moment when our eyes are opened,
and we "know" in whom we have believed,
when our whole being kneels in silence
before the Son of God.

BESIDE THE LAKE
John, Ch. 21

THE MIRACULOUS CATCH

There are seven of them. Seven disillusioned disciples.
The Lord is dead. Dead their illusions.
The awaited kingdom has not come.
They go back to their jobs.
The fishers of men become fishers of fish,
as though nothing had happened.

And now in this everyday life,
the Lord comes to find them.
He comes unknown, as a stranger.
From now on he will come incognito.
He is to be recognized by his acts.
"Children, have you any fish?" They answered, "No!"
In vain a night of trouble and work.
But now at his order they throw out the net again.
And the net is filled.
Then old memories come into focus, of other catches
made with him.
And suddenly they "know" it is he.

It is the beloved disciple—the one who never gives his name—who first recognizes the Lord. But it is Peter who jumps into the water.

Nights in this world when our faith wavers
and no longer believes in the Morning.
Cana, the miracle of the loaves and fishes, the miraculous catch: starvation and abundance.
Signs of God's fullness given to the church.

The mysterious host waits for his friends on the bank.
The meal is ready.
It will always be ready for us, through eternity.
"Jesus came and took the bread and gave it to them."

THE COMMISSION RENEWED

"Simon, son of John, do you love me more than these?"
"Simon": in this serious hour of rehabilitation, Jesus calls Peter by his old name.
—**"Yes, Lord, you know I love you."** The Greek word shows a new humility. No longer the Simon Peter so sure of himself. He claims no priority. But he loves the Lord: *it is true,* in all his poverty, he loves him!

Yes, Lord, what else can we say to you? In spite of all our unfaithfulness and our denials, *it is true,* we love you!

"Feed my lambs": Simon reinstated in his career as fisher of men, in his career as a shepherd to the Lord's flocks.

The question and the commission are repeated thrice, as the denial was triple.

160

And Peter, hurt by this triple reminder, bursts out:
"Lord, you know everything; you know that I love you."

Three times Jesus entrusts Simon Peter with the direction of his flock. He restores him, "publicly" as it were, to his calling as chief of the apostles.
But no greater than the others.
"Truly, truly, I say to you,
when you were young,
you girded yourself,
and walked where you would;
but when you are old,
you will strech out your hands,
and another will gird you
and lead you where you do not wish to go."
Simon, impulsive, is henceforth bound:
bound by his Lord,
bound by the Holy Spirit,
bound by men; led to martyrdom.

When you were young, you went where you wished. The day is coming when you will go where you do not want to: true, Lord, of every one of us.
Ways in which you lead us, which we would not have chosen.
The unknowns of tomorrow and the last agony.

Happy the man who, having entrusted his life to you, has nothing to fear for tomorrow.

And what about the one beside me?
Peter would like to know. I would like to know too . . .

"What is that to you? Follow me."

The beloved disciple's destiny, as his name, is not revealed.

The secret of every destiny, which we would always like to penetrate. One thing only is of any importance.

"FOLLOW ME."

EXPLANATORY AND
BIBLIOGRAPHICAL NOTES

* In John 1:5, the verb in Greek translated as "touched" or as "conquered" can mean "to grasp" in the figurative meaning of understanding a truth, or "to grasp" in the meaning of taking over, surmounting, conquering.

1. THE MILIEU, THE AUTHOR

The Fourth Gospel has always been a problem for its commentators, for it is different from the Synoptic Gospels both in style and content.

Johannine studies had a new impetus in the discovery of the manuscripts from Qumran and in the recent research done on the Jewish and Greek Gnostic sects at the end of the first century. The emphasis on "knowledge," the antinomies "light-darkness," "truth-lies," a certain mystical theology of unity, are characteristic of these milieux. And we find this language and these categories of thought in the Fourth Gospel. But the contrasts are all the more distinct. We feel that the author of this Gospel made very bold use of the vocabulary of his time to make the very unique character of the revelation he was conveying stand out even more clearly. For him there is only one Light, one Truth, one Savior of the world, Jesus Christ, the Word made flesh.

Who is the author of this extraordinary Gospel? According to a tradition going back to the second century, it is John the apostle, who died at a very old age at Ephesus.

163

It is interesting to note that the author is designated in the Gospel only as *"the disciple whom Jesus loved."* Another factor is that John, son of Zebedee, is never named. Undoubtedly a case of voluntary anonymousness.

The apostolic origin of the Fourth Gospel was strongly disputed by critics at a time when it was considered to be a work of the second century. Today, on the contrary, it is usually situated in the last quarter of the first century, and many of its historical aspects are regarded as valid.

For the study of this question:

PH. MENOUD, *L'Evangile de Jean d'après les recherches récentes* [The Gospel of John in the Light of Recent Research]. Delachaux et Niestlé, Neuchâtel and Paris, 1947— in the series Cahiers théologiques de l'Actualité protestante, No. 3.

See also the brief but excellent chapter on Johannine theology in SCHNACKENBURG, *La théologie du Nouveau Testament,* in Studio Neotestamentica, Desclée de Brouwer. [English translation: *Moral Teaching of the New Testament.* Herder & Herder.]

Although many studies have come out on one aspect or another of the Johannine message, we are still waiting for the solid, overall commentary which the French-language reading public needs.

Original works in English:

E. C. HOSKYNS and F. N. DAVEY, *The Fourth Gospel.* London: Faber & Faber, Ltd., 1947.

C. H. DODD, *The Fourth Gospel.* London: Cambridge University Press, 1954. Rather technical.

C. K. BARRETT, *The Gospel According to St. John.* London: S.P.C.K., 1955.

WILLIAM TEMPLE, *Readings in St. John's Gospel.* St. Martin's Press, Inc., 1955.

2. JESUS' TITLES IN THE FOURTH GOSPEL

a. SON OF MAN

In Hebrew and in Aramaic "son of man" may simply mean "man." In the Book of Daniel, the Son of Man ap-

164

pears at the end of time and the Ancient of Days confers royalty on him (Dan. 7:13). In the Judaism of Jesus' time, and especially in the Book of Enoch, the Son of Man is he whose name the Ancient of Days pronounced at the beginning of creation and he will come at the end of time to judge the world.

In the Synoptic Gospels the term is spoken by Jesus but never by his disciples, which leads us to think that he deliberately chose this term in preference to that of Messiah which was more easily misunderstood. In the Fourth Gospel, the term appears twelve times with a definitely Christological meaning. *"No one has ascended into heaven but he who descended from heaven, the Son of Man."* (John 3:13.) He is preexistent. His functions are those of a judge (John 5:27). He gives his flesh and blood for the life of the world (John 6:27,53,62–63). His "lifting up" is the decisive hour in the history of the world (John 3:14–15; 8:28; 12:31–34).

Concerning this question see:

O. CULLMANN, *Christologie du Nouveau Testament,* pp. 118 ff. and 159–162. [English translation: *The Christology of the New Testament,* tr. by Shirley C. Guthrie and Charles A. M. Hall; The Westminster Press, rev. ed., 1964.]

TH. PREISS, *Le Fils de l'homme* [The Son of Man], Montpellier, 1953, collection Etudes théologiques et religieuses.

b. THE WORD OR THE VERB (*Logos*)

This expression is found in its absolute form only in the Prologue. There has been much discussion as to its meaning. Some have seen in this word the influence of Gnostic circles of that time which considered the *logos* to be a mythological intermediary being between God and man. Others emphasize the importance of the Word in the Old Testament, especially in the story of creation, and concerning Wisdom (Prov. 8:22–26). But the Johannine message is precisely original in that the Logos for him is neither an abstraction nor a mythological being, but very clearly the incarnate Word in Jesus of Nazareth.

Concerning this question see:

165

O. CULLMANN, *op. cit.*, pp. 216 ff.; DODD, HOSKYNS, etc.

M. E. BOISMARD, o.p., *Le Prologue de St Jean,* in the collection Lectio Divina, Le Cerf.

c. THE SON OF GOD

In Judaism, the chosen people is sometimes called "the Son of God"; the kings also (Hos. 11:1; Isa. 1:2; II Sam. 7:14; Ps. 2:7); and that because of a particular calling. In the Synoptic Gospels, Jesus' Sonship is manifested in his perfect obedience to God's will, in the intimacy of his relationship with the Father. In the Fourth Gospel the divine Sonship of Jesus and its very uniqueness are constantly emphasized. "Only" is synonymous with "beloved." Johannine preaching openly proclaims this Sonship. The Son is submitted to the Father, but there is such identity that the Son can say: *"He who has seen me has seen the Father."* All of God's attributes, source of life and light, living water, and even the sacred name, are now attributes of the Son ("I am," Ex. 3:14). The supreme confession of faith is Thomas': My Lord and my God!

O. CULLMANN, *op. cit.,* pp. 234 ff. and the other commentaries mentioned.

d. THE LAMB OF GOD

The expression is only used twice and attributed to John the Baptist (John 1:29,36). Certain authors (Jeremias) emphasize the fact that in Aramaic the same word is used for lamb and servant, and see in this passage a reference to the Ebed Yahweh of Isa., ch. 53. Be this hypothesis right or wrong, the two expressions are similar since the Servant of Isaiah is compared to a dumb lamb (Isa. 53:7). Moreover, the idea of the paschal lamb is certainly present in the Gospel writer's mind: he situates Jesus' death on the fourteenth of Nisan, the day of preparation for the Passover, at the very hour when the lamb was customarily sacrificed. He emphasizes the fact that none of Christ's bones were broken on the cross (John 19:33–36; cf. Ex. 12:46; Num. 9:12; Ps. 34:20). This symbolism of the paschal lamb receives

166

a long development in Revelation. See also I Cor. 5:7; I Peter 1:19.

Although the notion of the servant appears explicitly only in John, ch. 13, it is implicit throughout the Gospel. Jesus freely gives his life for his own (John 10:11–18; 15:13). He is conscious of giving his flesh and blood for the life of the world (John 6:51).

According to Professor Cullmann, the words attributed to John the Baptist indicate the true meaning of Christian baptism as a baptism of the Spirit, but linked in with Christ's sacrifice, in such a way that there can only be one baptism in his death (in the sense of Rom., ch. 6).

The Gospel writer also has the task of refuting those who are still practicing John's baptism (cf. Acts 18:25; 19:1–5).

See O. CULLMANN, *Les Sacrements dans l'Evangile johannique* [The Sacraments in the Johannine Gospel], chapter entitled ".Jean-Baptiste et le baptême de Jésus." And *Christology du Nouveau Testament,* pp 64–65.

M. E. BOISMARD, *Du baptême à Cana* [On the Baptism at Cana], collection Lectio Divina, No. 18.

3. SACRAMENTAL CHARACTER

We emphasize in our studies the *sacramental* or *cultural* character of The Gospel According to John. Not only do the great Jewish feasts serve as chronological guideposts, but they are also used each time as a means of announcing the new form of worship "in spirit and in truth," as the church practices it. The material happening has a second meaning, a spiritual meaning, which in certain cases (the Cana wedding) is only hinted at, but in others explicitly stated (the miracle of the loaves and fishes) . Concerning this aspect we refer you to Professor Cullmann's important brochure, and on the Catholic side to Professor Feuillet's book:

O. CULLMANN, *Les Sacrements dans l'Evangile johannique,* Presses Universitaires de France, collection Etudes d'histoire et de philosophie religieuse.

A. FEUILLET, *Etudes johanniques,* Desclée de Brouwer. [English translation: *Johannine Studies.* Alba House.]

4. THE "SIGNS"

The Fourth Gospel uses the word "sign" to designate miracles, which points out that every one of these physical acts has a second meaning: they are means of revealing the new era which Jesus is inaugurating by his incarnation and their meaning will be fully understood only after his death and resurrection. The physical sign is generally followed by a talk or a discussion explaining its meaning. The healing of the paralytic manifests Jesus' power to give life, that of the man born blind is to point out the faith of some and the blindness of others. And so forth. (Dodd's commentary calls chapters 2 to 12:50 of the Gospel "The Book of Signs.")

5. THE TRIAL

The *juridical* character of the Fourth Gospel, the importance of the ideas of "witness," "accuser," "judgment" in the unfolding of the discussions between Jesus and the Pharisees, discussions considered as the inquiry of a trial, has been studied in a very thought-provoking way by THÉODORE PREISS, "La justification dans la pensée johannique," in *Vie en Christ,* Delachaux et Niestlé, Neuchâtel and Paris, 1951. [English translation: *Life in Christ,* tr. by H. Knight; Alec R. Allenson, Inc., 1957.]

6. THE HOUR

Someone's hour is when he accomplishes the work for which he was destined. Thus the woman's "hour" is when she gives birth (John 16:21). Jesus' "hour" is that of his death and glorification, for he came for that hour (ch. 12:27). The Gospel writer prepares us from the beginning for that hour, refers us to it, for nothing has any meaning except in terms of that fulfillment (John 2:4; 4:23; 5:25; 7:6,30; 8:20; 12:23,27; 13:1; 17:1).

On this point, see FEUILLET, *op. cit.,* the chapter "Jesus' Hour and the Wedding at Cana."

7. LIFE AND LIGHT

The two terms are very closely associated in this Gospel and make up its two essential themes (John 1:1–10).

The word "life" appears thirty-six times. God is the God of life. He sent his Son to give us life (John 3:16). The gospel was written that we might have life (John 20:31; cf. I John 1:1–2).

The Gospel speaks of "life" and of "life eternal" without making any distinction between the two. In either case the life has its origin in God. It is qualitatively different from purely physical life, it is on another plane: it is the life of the coming age. But it can be clearly seen from several passages that for John that life begins here and now, from the moment we meet Christ and believe his word (John 5:24–25; 10:27–28; 11:25–26).

The antinomy "light-darkness" is found in almost all religions and was very widespread in the first century: it is the most current symbol of the antinomy "life-death." It is also found in the Old Testament, but light is never deified there; it is according to Genesis the first creation of the Word of God (Gen. 1:3). For John it is that very Word, and its function is to *reveal:* it reveals God; it also reveals the reality of men and things, discovers them as truth or a lie (John 1:1–14; 3:16–21; 8:12; 9:4–5; 12:35–36). It is with this meaning that Jesus declares himself to be the Light of the World. (Concerning the "children of light," cf. Eph. 5:8–14; I John 1:5–7; 2:6–11.)

8. BELIEVING AND KNOWING

The two terms are very similar in John's language and are frequent terms in the Gnostic vocabulary of that time. It is thus worthwhile to search out their most exact meaning. Believing, for John, is recognizing in Jesus the One sent of God, is receiving his word, "seeing his glory." The Gospel thus sets constantly over against each other those who "believe" and those who "do not believe." Believing is believing "in his name" (John 1:12; 3:18; 4:42; 5:24; 7:5; 8:24;

10:37–38; 11:40). The Greek word "to know" is found forty-seven times in the Fourth Gospel; but it is sometimes translated in . . . [our languages] by other verbs for knowing such as "recognizing," "understanding." It can designate an objective knowledge (he "knew," John 2:25), the understanding of the true meaning of a word or event (ch. 8:27), the knowledge of faith ("we believe and we know," John 6:69), and especially knowledge-communion (John 10:14–15,27; 17:3,25–26).

"To know" in John's vocabulary presupposes a mutual gift of self: it is being loved and loving. But loving God, as in the Old Testament, is also doing his will (Hos. 4:2; Isa. 1:2; Jer. 31:33–34; John 8:31–32).

Concerning this question see:

La connaissance de Dieu selon le N.T. et son milieu [The Knowledge of God According to the N.T. and Its Milieu], in Cahiers Bibliques, No. 3, especially the article by Professor PIERRE BONNARD, "Connaître Dieu selon le quatrième Evangile et la gnose hellénistique" [Knowing God According to the Fourth Gospel and Hellenistic Gnosticism] (*Foi et Vie*, 1965).

9. SYMBOLISM

a. WATER

Concerning living water (John 4:3–15; 7:37–39; cf. Zech. 14:8; Ezek., ch. 47), see in Cahiers Bibliques, No. 3, the article by A. JAUBERT on "Symbolique de l'eau et connaissance de Dieu" [The Symbolism of Water and the Knowledge of God].

b. BREAD

See A. FEUILLET, *op. cit.*, Ch. III.

10. TRUTH

The Greek word means etymologically "that which is not hidden," whence a notion of reality, of authenticity, of veracity, and also of revelation. In the Fourth Gospel, Jesus reveals not only truth, he is himself the truth. It is no question of an intellectual category as in Greek thought: truth is reached only by the obedience of faith (John 8:31–32), by a living union with him who is Truth (John 14:5–7).

11. GLORY

This term appears constantly in the Fourth Gospel. In Hebrew tradition, glory is the visible manifestation of God's presence, and several texts emphasize that for men it is unbearable (Ex. 33:18–23; I Kings 8:10; Isa. 6:1–5). Glory is associated with the notion of light, of luminous radiation. The Greek word used in the New Testament to translate the Hebrew has a secular meaning of opinion or reputation.

In the Fourth Gospel the word occasionally has its ordinary Greek meaning (John 5:41,44; 7:18; 12:42–43). But Christ's glory is essentially found in the gift of his life for the salvation of men. He "glorifies" the Father, that is, he manifests his redeeming love by dying on the cross; and the Father "glorifies" his Son by resurrecting him from the dead, by recognizing him as his (John 12:23–28; 17:1–5). It is said of his disciples that they *see his glory,* that is, his majesty and his real power under the human envelope still hiding them (John 2:11; 11:40). The disciples glorify him by their witnessing (ch. 17:10) and will participate in his glory (ch. 17:22–26). This glory is in the Fourth Gospel *a view of faith.*

12. JESUS' LAST TALK WITH HIS DISCIPLES (CHS. 13 TO 16)

See, besides the commentaries already mentioned:

H. van der Bussche, *Le Discours d'adieu de Jésus* [Jesus' Last Talk with His Disciples], Castermann, 1959 (Bible et Vie chrétienne).

A. Feuillet, *Johannine Studies,* the chapter "The Time for the Church."

171